Enter If You Dare...

BOOK FOUR
How To Haunt Your House

Copyright

Copyright © 2014 by Shawn and Lynne Mitchell
Pensacola, Florida www.howtohauntyourhouse.com

Published by Rabbit Hole Productions
www.rabbitholeproductions.com

All rights reserved. No part of this book may be reproduced or transmitted in any form or by any means, electronic or mechanical, including photocopying, recording, or by any information storage and retrieval system, without permission in writing from the authors.

Library of Congress Cataloging-in-publication Data
How To Haunt Your House, Book Four
/ Shawn and Lynne Mitchell

ISBN 978-0-9856304-6-1 (paperback)

Notice: Authors and publisher make no representation, warranty or guarantee that the techniques or information described in this book will be safe for the reader or visitors in any situation or under any conditions. Authors and publisher accept no responsibility for any injury resulting from the application or any technique described or shown in this book.

How To Haunt Your House 4
CONTENTS

08 Flying Phantasms

24 Around the Cauldron Fire

28 Lab Bubblers

34 Designing the Mad Lab Set

40 Build a Creepy Forest

48 Filler Spiders

56 Beef Netting Spider Webs

60 Motion Activated Spider

66 Web Victims

70 Jointed-Leg Spider

76 Toxic Scene & Kicking Leg Spider

82 Making An Entrance

88 Inside the Haunted House

95 Other Resources

96 Website

Flying Phantasms
Dancing Bride & Groom

The spectral glow of the twilight lovers can be glimpsed hovering over the tombstones on All Hallows Eve. Their silent dance is eternal, touching, and tragic. Having lost each other in life, they reunite once again in death.

YOU WILL NEED: Phantoms- Any kind of plastics that are clear or white, craft wire, packing tape, packing plastic wrap, scissors, fishing line, large sewing needle, manikin forms for male, female, or child, hot glue gun, glue sticks, utility knife, plastic Poly Tubing on a roll for the air bag in sizes 2 inch and 3 inch wide, heat sealer (Impulse Sealer), gift shrink wrap roll, small UV spotlights, blue bulb shop light, heat gun, ceiling fan pole (threaded on one end), Styrofoam head form, white and black duct tape, plastic grocery bags, white spray paint, face masks, pipe cleaners, faux white roses, white netting fabric, any white decorative fabric or trim that is translucent, drinking straw, white wig (for female), white gloves (male), long white gloves (female), white child gloves, 4-way metal pipe, screws, PVC pipe, PVC pipe cutters, 4 way PVC connectors, PVC glue, translucent sheet plastic (male hat), Christmas tree turner

Packing tape ghosts are fairly common online. We were trying to come up with a similar effect using less tape and more plastic that would stand up to the elements better and be able to support its own weight.

LIGHT TEST: Using a blue shop light shine light from behind the plastic shell. Here white netting was also added over the top of the plastic.

Air Bag with slit cut in end and plastic tie inserted.

5 Cut open the plastic layers along the back of the manikin. Remove from form. Use packing tape to close the cut and reshape new body form.

6 Creating the air bag limbs: Cut a length of the 3 inch plastic tube bag. This will go through the body and form both arms. Using the heat sealer, seal one end of the 3 inch bag. The goal is not to over fill these with air. They will need to be foldable at several points. Too much air will pop the bag when folded. Seal the opposite end leaving a 1/2 inch opening. Insert a drinking straw into the opening. Blow some air into the bag. Pinch closed and see if the tube can be folded. Release some air if needed. Seal the remaining opening. Create three identical air bags. These will form the arms.

Head Process

1 Loosely drape shrink wrap material over head. Tape at sides.

2 Use heat gun to shrink material around head shape.

3 Wrap packing plastic around the head form 4-6 times.

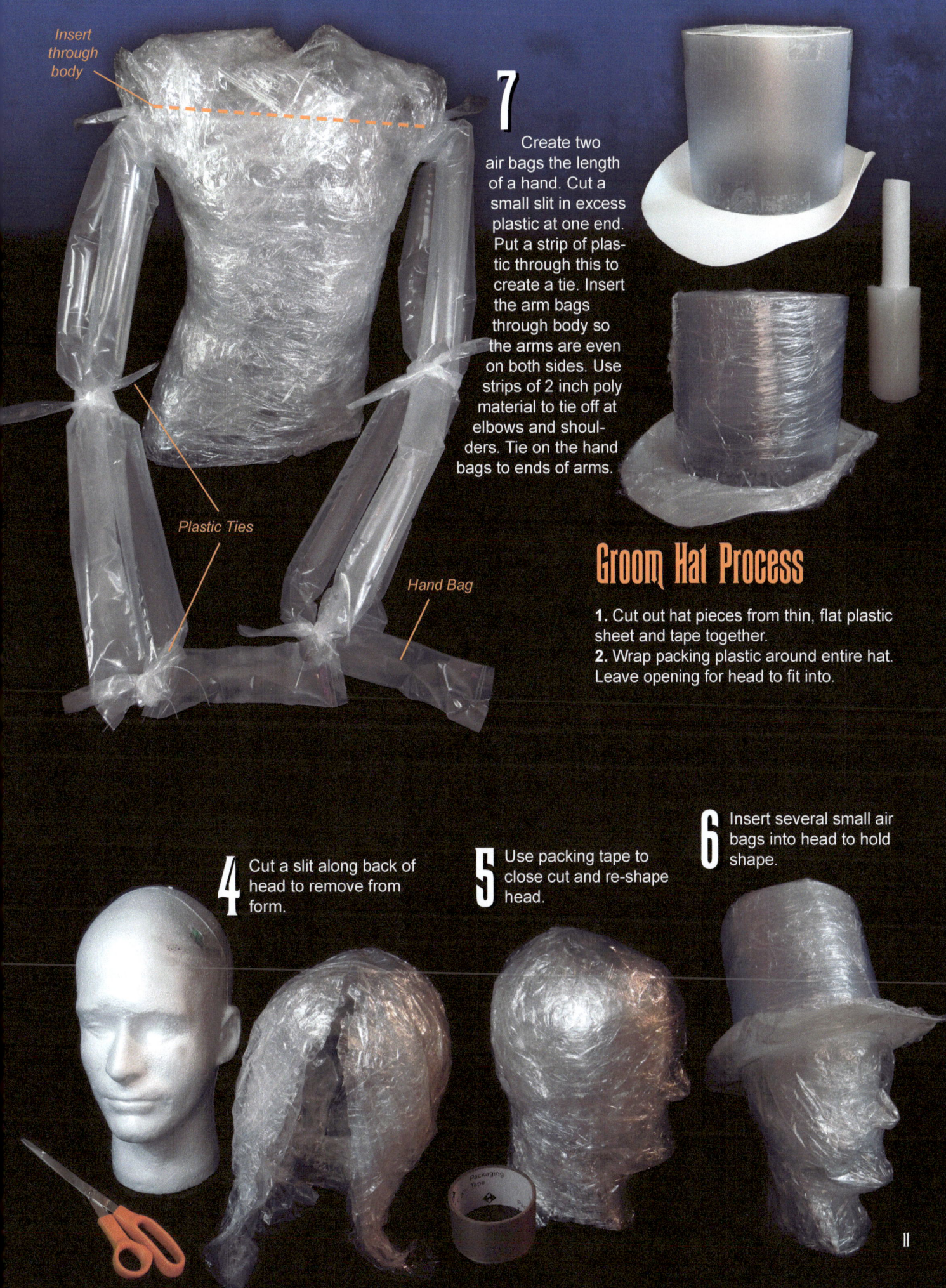

Insert through body

Plastic Ties

Hand Bag

7 Create two air bags the length of a hand. Cut a small slit in excess plastic at one end. Put a strip of plastic through this to create a tie. Insert the arm bags through body so the arms are even on both sides. Use strips of 2 inch poly material to tie off at elbows and shoulders. Tie on the hand bags to ends of arms.

Groom Hat Process

1. Cut out hat pieces from thin, flat plastic sheet and tape together.
2. Wrap packing plastic around entire hat. Leave opening for head to fit into.

4 Cut a slit along back of head to remove from form.

5 Use packing tape to close cut and re-shape head.

6 Insert several small air bags into head to hold shape.

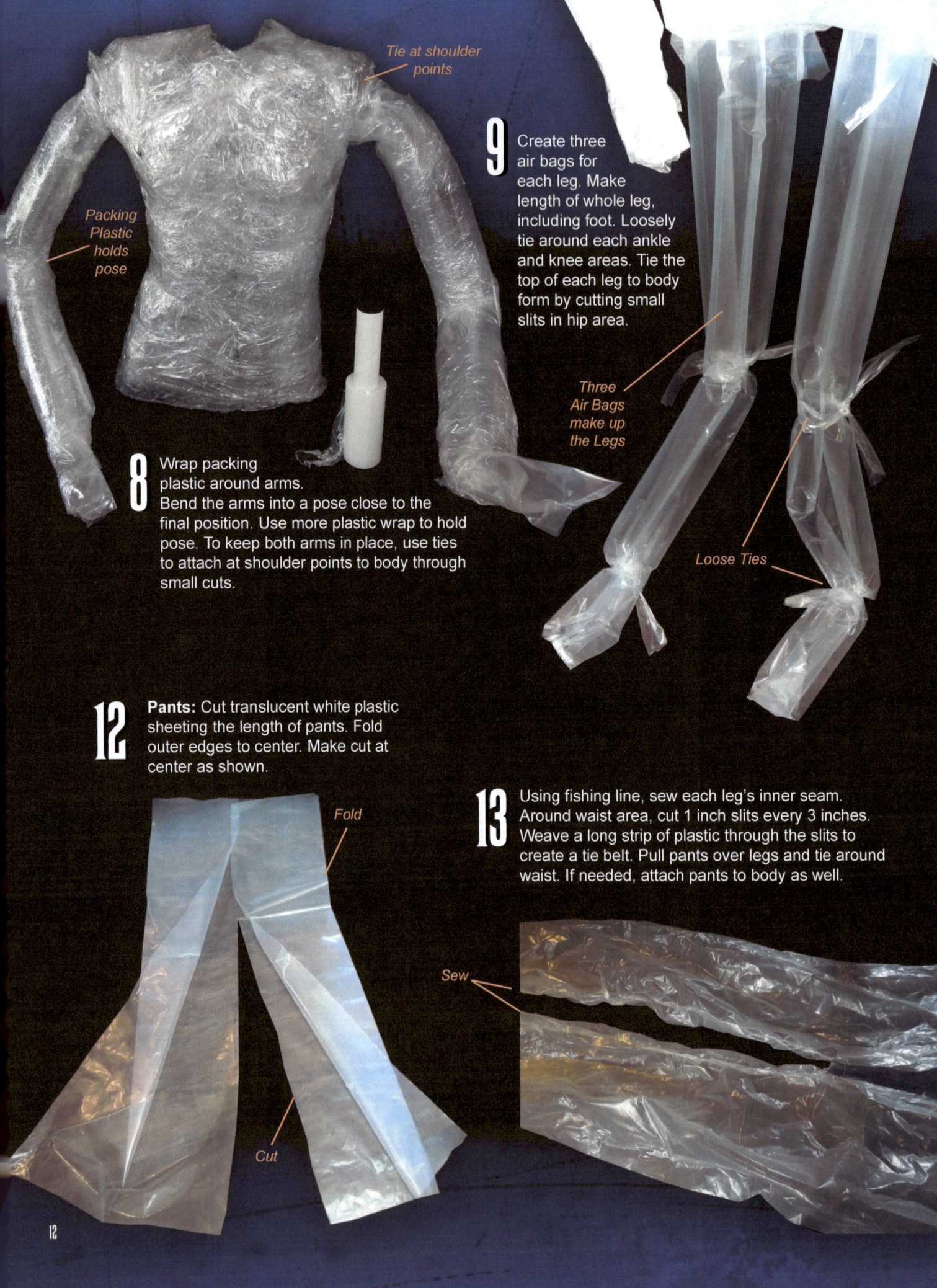

10 Bend each leg and foot into final pose and wrap in packing plastic.

11 Create air bag that is twice the length of the neck. Fold in half and insert in head. Wrap in packing plastic. Face mask is spray painted white. Once dry, attach with mask elastic around head.

14 Sleeves: Cut length of plastic for each arm leaving enough at end to fold up as a cuff. Sew along length same method as legs. Make a small slit at top of sleeve shoulder. Slide sleeve over each arm and attach to body with plastic tie.

Sew

Cuff

Fold

Body with Sleeves and Pants attached

15 Coat front: Cut translucent white plastic sheeting in the shape of a vest front as shown. Using white, duct tape, create the vest lapels. Add two duct tape strips as the pocket tops as well. Attach by cutting two small slits at sides and tie around waist of body. Sew or tie to tops of shoulders also.

16 Coat Tails: Cut two layers of translucent white plastic sheeting in shape shown. Cut a single piece of strong craft wire that will wrap around outside edges and half way up inside edges. Sandwich the wire between the two sheets. Tape or sew the plastic edges to the wire. Create two slits near top for ties. Attach these to body. Twist wired tail ends to curl up and away from body.

17 Hands: Bend five pipe cleaners in half. Bunch up five pieces of plastic the length of a finger. Twist a pipe cleaner around each piece of plastic. Bind the ends of all finger pieces together at one end. Insert this into glove. Add more plastic to hand to fill out. Do same for other glove. Slide each glove over ends of each arm. Attach with plastic ties.

White Netting Fabric Overlay

18 Coat Cape: Cut enough translucent white plastic to go around back and shoulders. Loosely gather top edge of cape using fishing line. Cut a long rectangle for coat stand-up collar. Fold this in half and sew to cape along top edge. Cut a piece of distressed, white netting same size as cape. Sew this over plastic cape at base of collar.

Stand-up Collar

Coat Tail wire bent up on ends

Bride Body

1 Follow body steps same as male, this time using the female manikin.

2 Create a series of air bag rings (smaller to larger) that are attached end to end. Tie each ring together, starting at waist, leaving space between each using plastic ties as shown. This will help keep the bride's skirt flared out.

3 Create similar air bag structure for large Victorian Sleeve Puffs. Tie loosely around the neck and under arms.

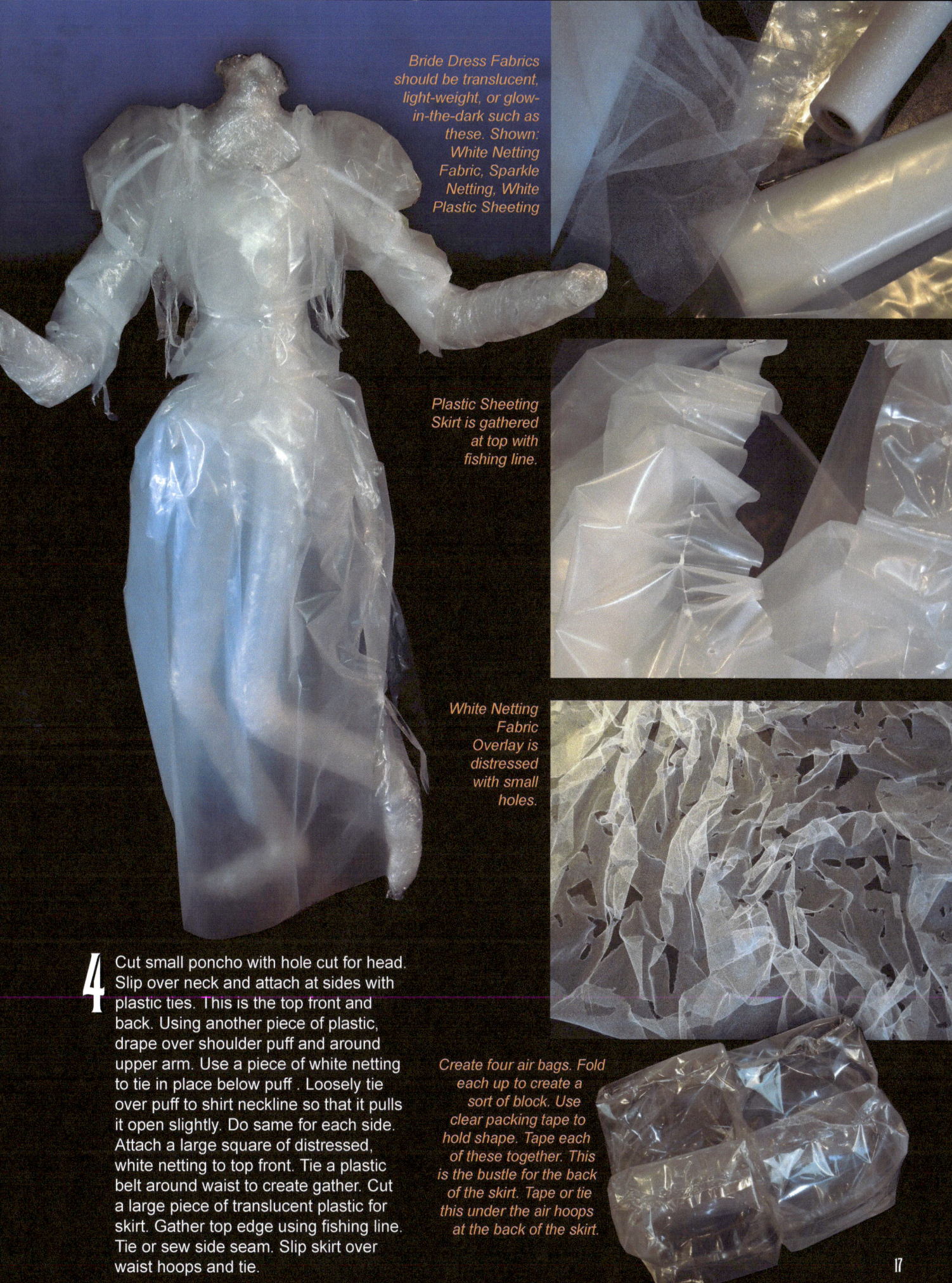

Bride Dress Fabrics should be translucent, light-weight, or glow-in-the-dark such as these. Shown: White Netting Fabric, Sparkle Netting, White Plastic Sheeting

Plastic Sheeting Skirt is gathered at top with fishing line.

White Netting Fabric Overlay is distressed with small holes.

4 Cut small poncho with hole cut for head. Slip over neck and attach at sides with plastic ties. This is the top front and back. Using another piece of plastic, drape over shoulder puff and around upper arm. Use a piece of white netting to tie in place below puff. Loosely tie over puff to shirt neckline so that it pulls it open slightly. Do same for each side. Attach a large square of distressed, white netting to top front. Tie a plastic belt around waist to create gather. Cut a large piece of translucent plastic for skirt. Gather top edge using fishing line. Tie or sew side seam. Slip skirt over waist hoops and tie.

Create four air bags. Fold each up to create a sort of block. Use clear packing tape to hold shape. Tape each of these together. This is the bustle for the back of the skirt. Tape or tie this under the air hoops at the back of the skirt.

5 **Bride Head:** Create head similar to grooms. Add a female mask spray painted white. Style a white wig for bride. Sew or tie wig to head. Create a ring of faux white roses and a distressed veil of white netting. Attach this to wig.

6 Create several pieces of distressed, white netting. These will go over the skirt, top, and sleeves. The effect should be an old, moth-eaten wedding dress. Tie panels around body as needed. Add any other decorative accents for effect.

7 Create hands using pipe cleaners same as groom. Add these to long, white gloves and slip over bride arms.

8 Cut ends of plastic sleeves and skirt as torn ends.

Completed Bride Ghost ready for her eternal dance

The Bride & Groom Stand

Fabric and Plastics that have translucent or glow-in-the-dark properties work best for these ghosts!

Each light points at one of the ghosts suspended above it.

Christmas Tree Turner

Slowly rotates 360 degrees

1 Thread 4-way metal connector to ceiling fan extension rod. Insert the PVC pipe through center of connect so it is even on both sides. Secure in place with two screws through center hole. Add two 4-way PVC connectors to each end using PVC glue. Make sure they are both pointing upwards at a 90 degree angle.

2 Insert the bottom of the pipe into the Christmas tree turner. Extra padding may need to be added to keep it from shifting (Something like popsicle sticks could be taped around end to add extra bulk).

3 Use black duct tape to attach two small, LED UV spotlights at base of pole pointing up. Plug these into the stand. These LED spotlights are safe to use near the fabric and plastic as they do not produce any heat. They will give the ghosts an inner illumination as they slowly turn.

4 Cut a length of PVC pole that will reach from the figures neck to the 4-way connector.

5 Insert pole into figure body so that it goes from the front waist, through the chest and out at the back of the neck.

6 Use white duct tape to secure at neck. Do same for bride and groom.

PVC Pole inserted into back and up to neck

PVC Pole at waist will insert into 4-way connector at top of pole.

Secure neck pole with white duct tape around neck.

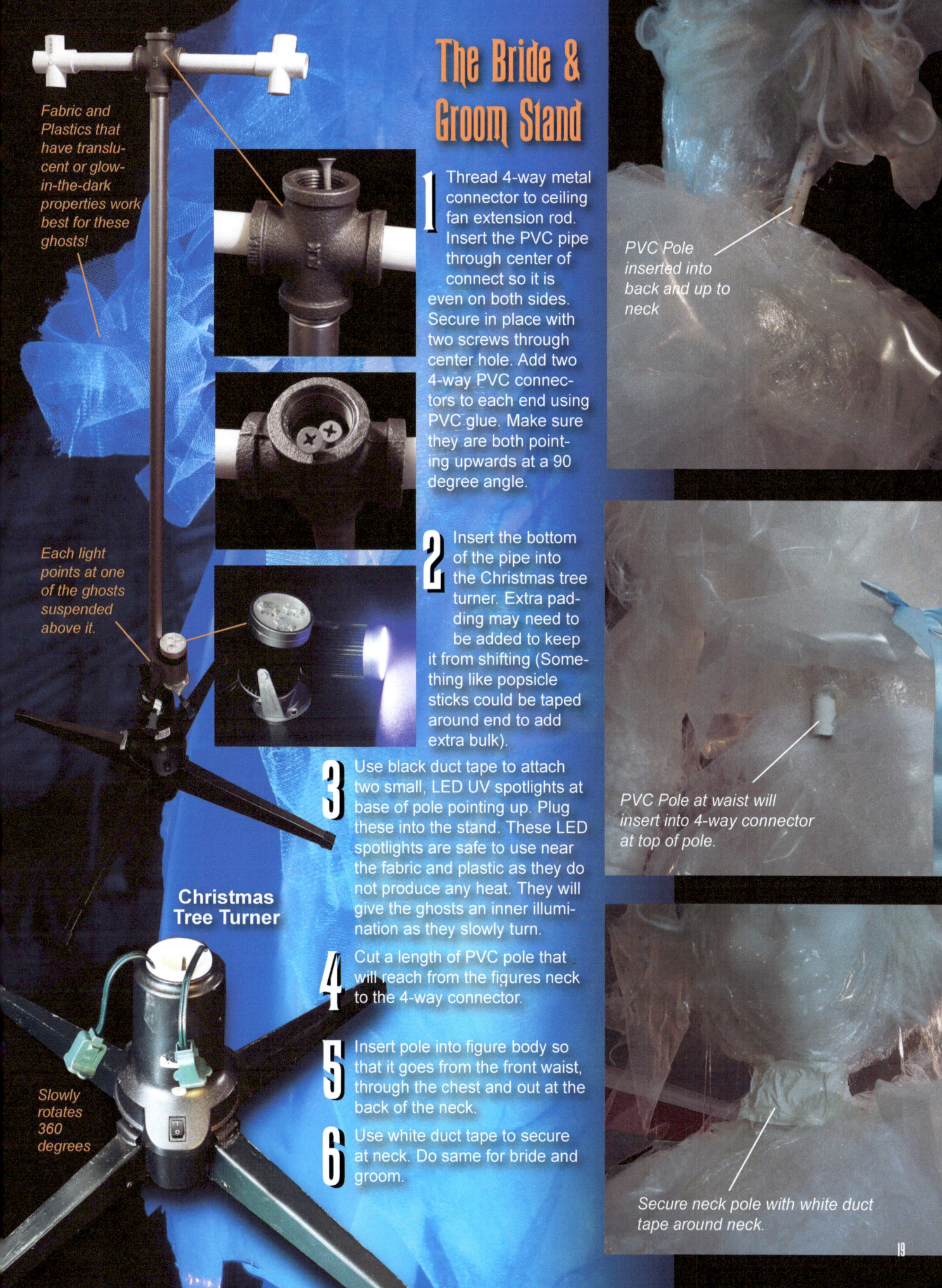

7 Insert body pole into 4-way connectors so the two figures face each other. DO NOT glue these poles to stand. You will want to be able to separate them when not on display.

8 Arrange figures arms around each other, as though dancing. Pose fingers as needed. Use fishing line, if needed, to secure poses.

9 **Positioning prop in graveyard:** Place heavy stones on Christmas tree turner arms. Hide external lights inside of urns or other props and point up at figures. Back lights work really well in this effect. Use tombstones to hide stand base and block view of lights.

The ghosts are semi-transparent overall with a few places that block more light. This helps drive the "ghost" effect of partially materialized.

10 Turn on to test. Figures should turn freely over tops of tombstones without getting caught on anything.

Ghosts glided over the walkway over the heads of guests.

White craft mask was added for the eerie face features.

The hands were simply the ends of the air-bags wrapped in plastic wrap. Child's gloves could also be used.

Suspension poles seen during the day.

Child-sized Ghosts

Smaller ghost versions can be made using the child form. Here two ghost girls were used. Each was posed as if they were floating in the air. One girl wears a bonnet hat. The other has long curls and a large hair bow. The curls were made by wrapping shrinkwrap around a card board tube and heating it with a heat gun. Remove the card board and the curls hold their form.

In this effect, the Christmas tree turner rotated a black rod attached at the top from which the ghosts were suspended on fishing line. The center pole was extended with a second pole to double its height. This was displayed near a walk-way so the ghost girls appeared to glide overhead. LED UV lights were pointed at each ghost so they always had a light facing them as they turned.

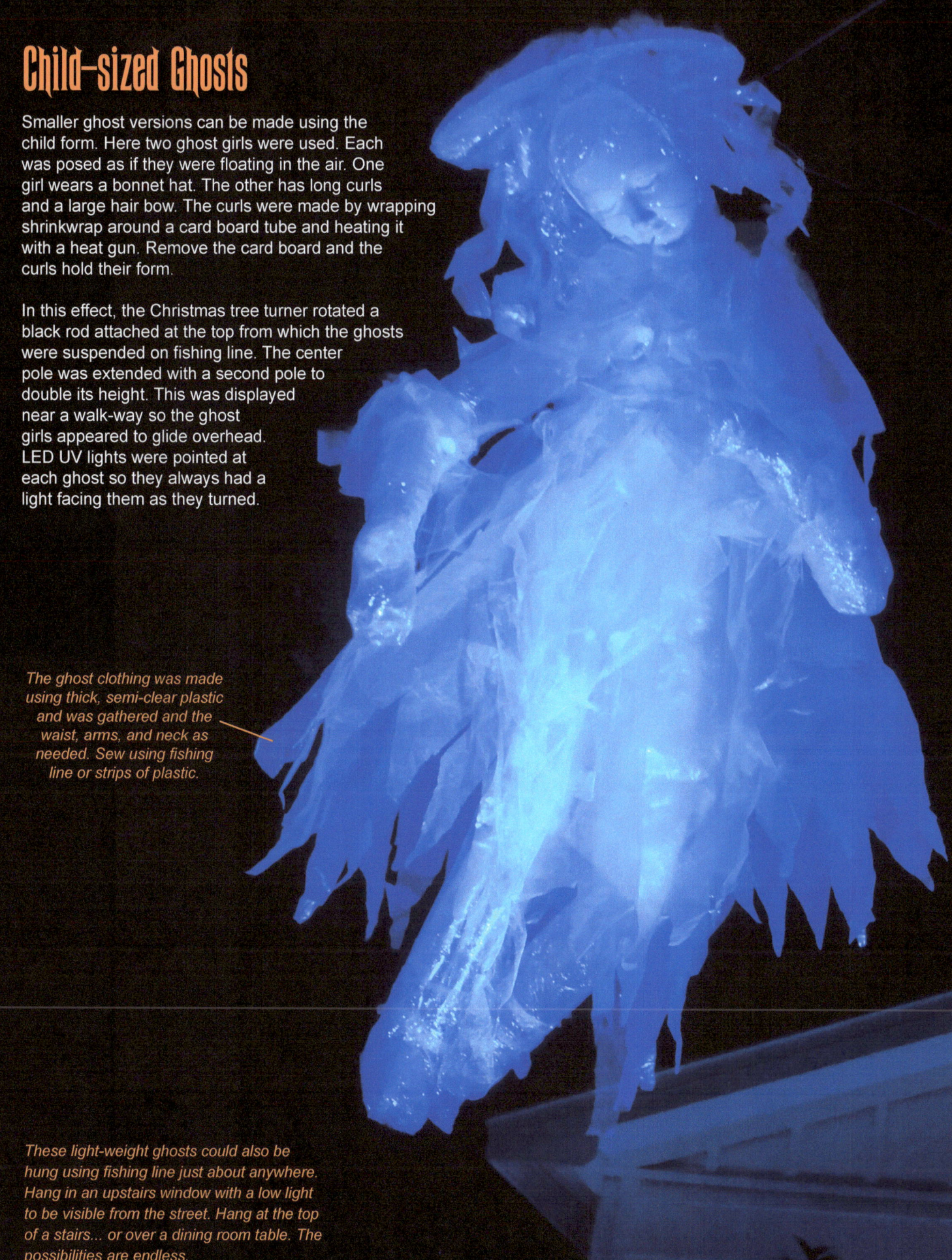

The ghost clothing was made using thick, semi-clear plastic and was gathered and the waist, arms, and neck as needed. Sew using fishing line or strips of plastic.

These light-weight ghosts could also be hung using fishing line just about anywhere. Hang in an upstairs window with a low light to be visible from the street. Hang at the top of a stairs... or over a dining room table. The possibilities are endless.

Around the Cauldron Fire

YOU WILL NEED: Thick Styrofoam pieces, hot tool for cutting Styrofoam, serrated knife, yellow, orange, brown, gray, and black craft paint, paint brush, plastic cauldrons, LED Christmas tree lights in yellow or red, Monster Mud, black duct tape, wire or coat hanger, cheap plastic cauldrons of various sizes, utility knife, Saran wrap, spray foam

"Double, double toil and trouble; Fire burn, and cauldron bubble"

1 Using a hot tool or serrated knife, carve various sizes of Styrofoam wood pieces. Leave high and low areas with jagged silhouettes. Small holes can also be added to allow the "fire-light" to show through.

2 For wood pieces that will be in the hot coals paint with the colors shown. First, paint orange for the hottest part of the wood.

3 Blend in the orange with yellow paint.

4 Add some more orange highlights as needed for contrast. Let dry.

5 Lastly, dry brush over the raised areas with black paint. Let dry.

Original Plastic Cauldron

Monster Mud applied to outside

Painted in Brown and cracks cut

6 On larger pieces of wood, hollow out the backside and create several small holes that will light through to the front side.

7 Various paint schemes can be used- from charred, black logs to burning logs with hot embers showing through. Create a variety for the cauldron fire pit using the ones shown here as inspiration.

8 Cauldrons: Using cheap, plastic cauldrons as a starting point cover the outside of the cauldron with Monster Mud. The texture should be applied in a thin, uneven layer. Let dry in the sun.

9 Paint over the Monster Mud layer with brown paint. Use a knife or hot tool to cut "cracks" along the cauldron lip. Cut small hole on two sides of the cauldron. Insert a piece of wire to form a handle. Twist ends to hold in place.

10 Mix black paint in water and let drip down sides of cauldron over brown paint.

11 Cover wire handle with black Duct Tape. Bunch up the tape as it is applied so it has a grungier appearance.

12 Hot Coals: Using an upside down cauldron or other similar rounded shape, cover with saran wrap. Spray expanding foam around sides in small round sizes as if "coals". Leave top area open. A few open holes are desirable in and around the coals. Let harden.

13 Remove shape from cauldron. Place on sheet of plastic. Continue to create Spray foam coats that spread out from base. Place in a few pieces of faux wood. Let harden.

14 Paint orange into the crevices of the Spray foam. Once dry, apply a light wash of black paint over the high points of the coals. It should look gray. Let dry. Last, paint black over a few areas of the coals on high points.

Tape-wrapped handle

15 In the haunt setting, place red or yellow LED Christmas lights underneath the coal pile. Add any remaining faux wood pieces and arrange cauldrons on top. Once lit, the lights will simulate a real cauldron fire.

Lab Bubblers

YOU WILL NEED: An assortment of PVC parts similar to those shown with a PVC Flange for base, as long as the parts fit together and stand on its own it should work. 12 inch wooden disk, ¾ Female Brass Sillcock Valve, 1 inch & ¼ inch rubber tubing, bright green, black, Glow in the Dark, & copper craft paint, silver & copper spray paint, assortment of gauges, clear plastic tube (we use a golf ball set that came in a long, clear tube, then repurpose the tube to make it water tight), paste-on eyes, ¼ inch brass snaps (hobby supply), fish tank bubble wall tube, fish tank filter pump, Silicone Sealant, universal check valve for fish tank pump, hot glue gun, hot glue sticks, ½ inch hole drill bit, ¼ drill bit, rubber stopper, painters tape, screws, drill, utility knife, food colouring, water, any other accessories you want to add

These industrial looking devices are perfect for the mad scientist laboratory. They are filled with colored liquids. They bubble and make creepy bubbling noises. They are painted to look as if they are corroded and well-used. All manner of valves, gauges, and tubes can be attached to extend their evil function.

Lab Bubblers can be designed or accessorized in all sorts of ways. This design is just to give you an idea of how to start.

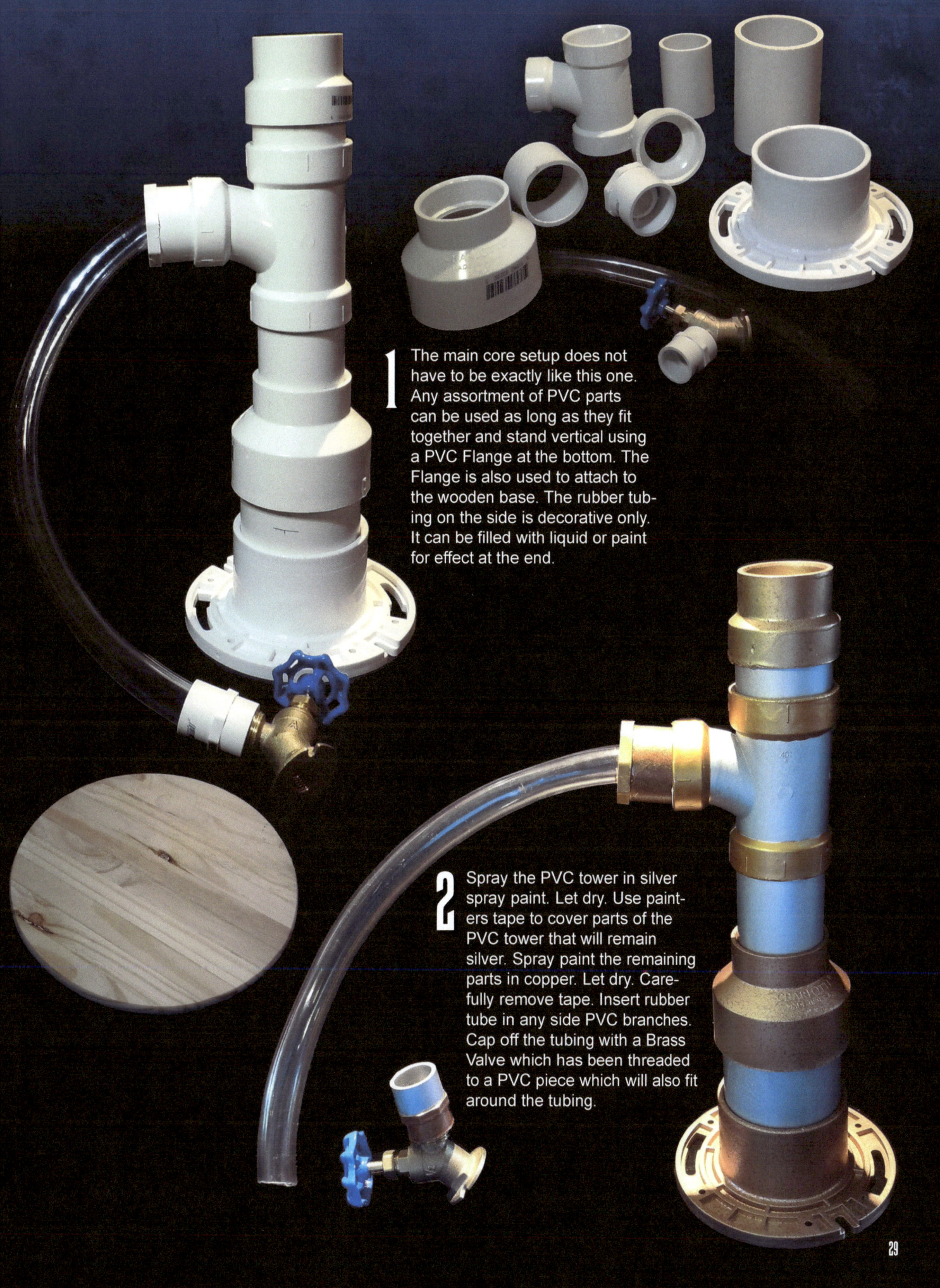

1. The main core setup does not have to be exactly like this one. Any assortment of PVC parts can be used as long as they fit together and stand vertical using a PVC Flange at the bottom. The Flange is also used to attach to the wooden base. The rubber tubing on the side is decorative only. It can be filled with liquid or paint for effect at the end.

2. Spray the PVC tower in silver spray paint. Let dry. Use painters tape to cover parts of the PVC tower that will remain silver. Spray paint the remaining parts in copper. Let dry. Carefully remove tape. Insert rubber tube in any side PVC branches. Cap off the tubing with a Brass Valve which has been threaded to a PVC piece which will also fit around the tubing.

6 Use copper paint on any gauges that will be attached. Let dry. Dab a little green paint along the edges and seams for a patina effect. Let dry.

7 Golf ball tube as it was purchased minus the golf balls.

Any kind of gauges can be used to ramp up the look!

8 Remove the top tube plug. Cut the tube plug off completely using a utility knife.

9 Spray paint the bottom plug with copper. Let dry.

Top tube plug with string

Top tube plug cut off

Bottom plug becomes the top

Original Color

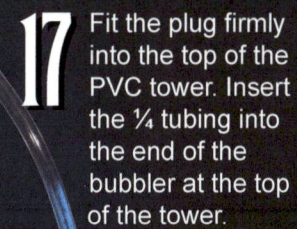

17 Fit the plug firmly into the top of the PVC tower. Insert the ¼ tubing into the end of the bubbler at the top of the tower.

Plug

18 To prevent back-siphoning of water, add a universal check valve to the ¼ tubing extending out of the top plug of the PVC tower.

Decorative only tubing with paint inside

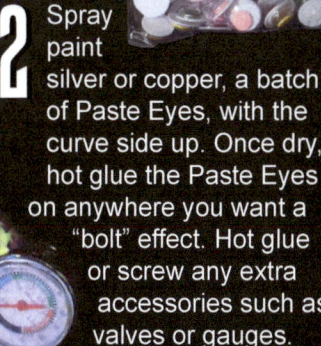

22 Spray paint silver or copper, a batch of Paste Eyes, with the curve side up. Once dry, hot glue the Paste Eyes on anywhere you want a "bolt" effect. Hot glue or screw any extra accessories such as valves or gauges.

19 Carefully fill the area over the plug and around the check valve with hot glue to prevent any leaks.

23 Attach the end of the ¼ tubing to a small fish tank pump. Pour small amount of water into the golf ball tube. Check for leaks. Add more sealant as needed. Once all leaks have been fixed, fill the tube completely with water and add a few drops of food color (any color). Replace top cap and plug in pump to test bubbler.

20 Use Silicone Sealant to attach the golf ball tube into the top. Mix some extra sealant with the green paint and apply over some of the green drip areas for grungier look. Let sealant dry overnight.

Silicone Sealant

21 Screw base of PVC tower to center of wood piece. This will keep it from tipping over. Drip more paint over these edges. If there are extra ¼ tubes being used for decoration, add some of the Glow in the Dark paint to the inside before attaching.

Designing The Mad Lab Set

Every good set design evolves from knowing the story that needs to be told and the use of layers. From small details to large, every part of a scene must propel the story in some way. Big set pieces are what the audience notices first. They instantly set the mood. But then, little by little, they discover the smaller elements. Here the story becomes cemented in believability. Now the audience is IN the story. It's a real place with real things that make sense.

From science apparatus to body parts the *Mad Lab* tells a story of experimentation, study, and reanimation.

Face Mask

Prop hand on a doll stand

Microscope

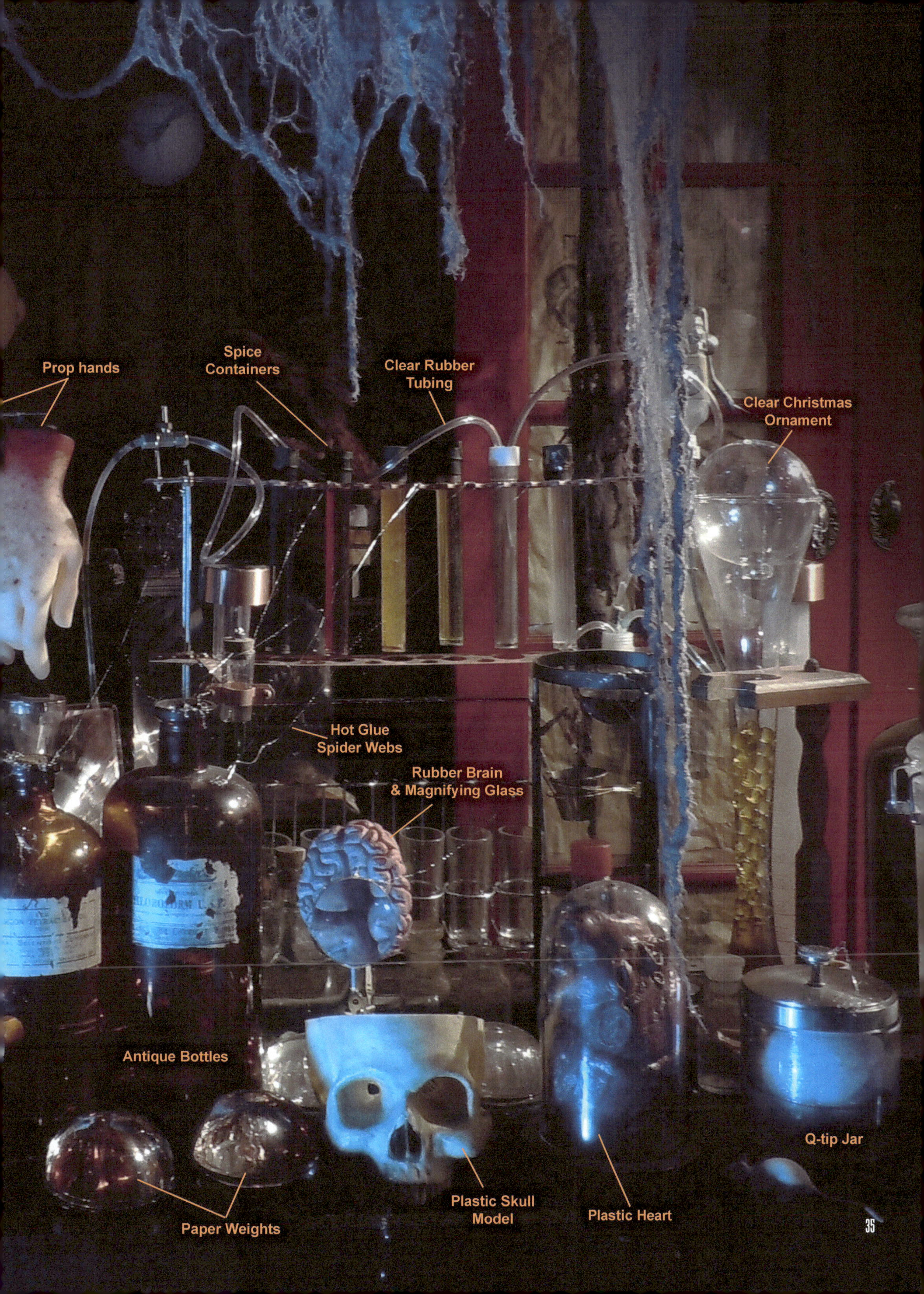

- Prop hands
- Spice Containers
- Clear Rubber Tubing
- Clear Christmas Ornament
- Hot Glue Spider Webs
- Rubber Brain & Magnifying Glass
- Antique Bottles
- Q-tip Jar
- Paper Weights
- Plastic Skull Model
- Plastic Heart

① *A Brain Bubblier (from **How to Haunt Your House, Book Three**) sits among test tubes and microscopes.*

② *A collection of natural specimens-- a mummy head, taxidermy spiders, snake skin, and insects bring a museum quality to the lab.*

③ *But, legitimate science gives way to fringe experiments. Ancient bottles of unknown liquids sit next to glass domes covering severed head and hands.*

④ *Hide small lights behind glass for best effect. Keep overall lighting dim or at low angles to make good use of shadows and unease.*

⑤ *Shelves of medical equipment and viles filled with different colours show a work in progress. Behind these is an old school caulk board inscribed with formulas and notes.*

6 Collections similar to this can be purchased online. It comes already framed and ready to display.

7 Every scientist might begin experimenting on mice, but eventually they move on to bigger, unwilling test subjects.

8 Just about any prop, such as this headhunter's trophy, when caged makes it seem still alive and potentially dangerous.

9 The sound activated animatronic figure is wrapped in chains. His electrically charged life is brief as he reaches toward the audience.

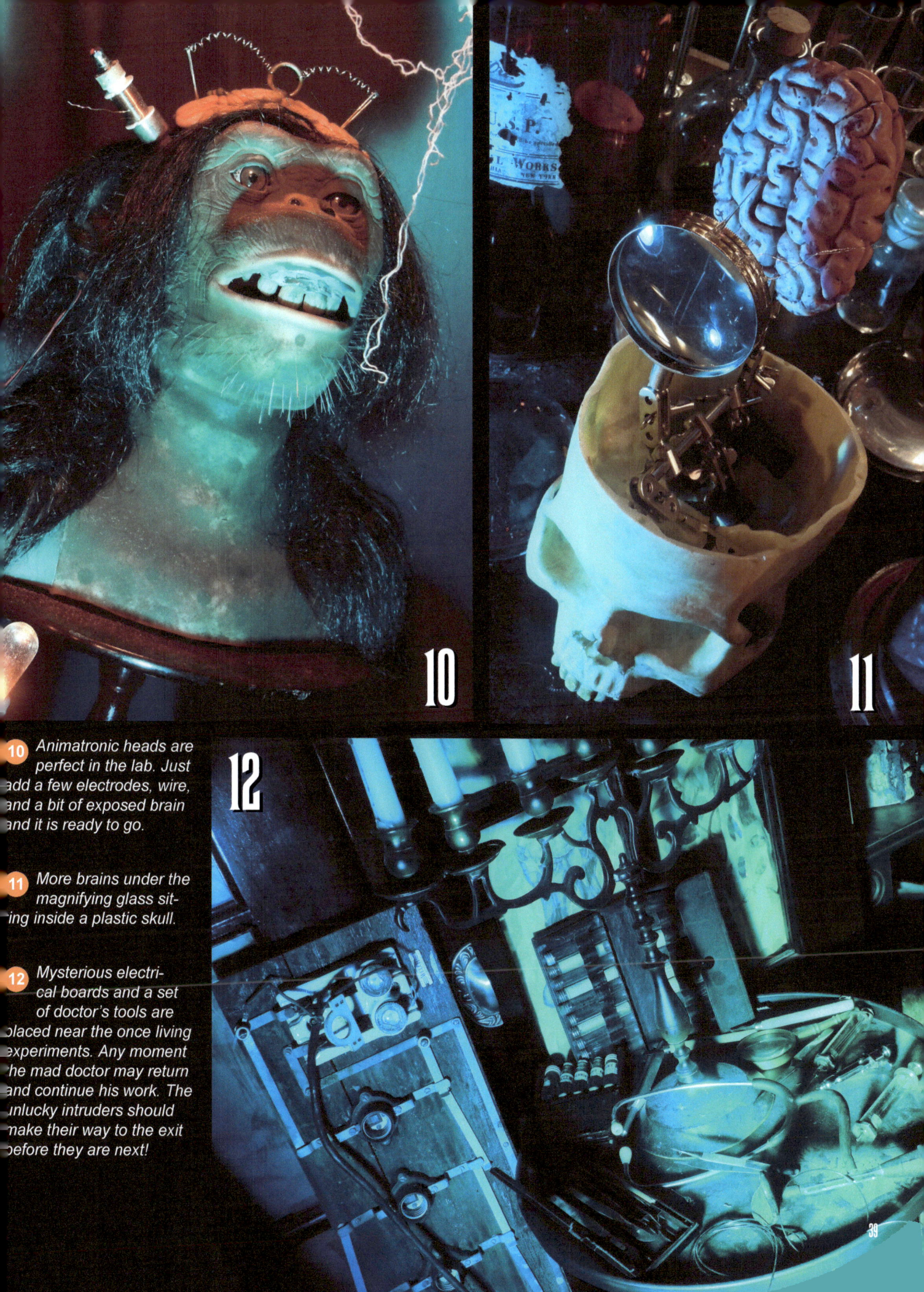

10 Animatronic heads are perfect in the lab. Just add a few electrodes, wire, and a bit of exposed brain and it is ready to go.

11 More brains under the magnifying glass sitting inside a plastic skull.

12 Mysterious electrical boards and a set of doctor's tools are placed near the once living experiments. Any moment the mad doctor may return and continue his work. The unlucky intruders should make their way to the exit before they are next!

Build A Creepy Forest
10 Foot Tall Trees

Not everyone is lucky enough to have the perfect, creepy trees, in exactly the right spots, for their Halloween display. But what if you could make them and put them just where you need them? We had this dilemma and this is what we came up with.

YOU WILL NEED: 4 inch round PVC pipe (10 foot long), ½ round PVC pipe, 1 ¼ inch round PVC pipe, heat gun, wet rag, clamps, screws, drill, several cans of spray foam, hammer, 1/8 drill bit, PVC cutter, black exterior house paint (gallon for 6 trees), brown craft paint, paint brush, 5 foot metal pole, thin tree branches, Spanish moss (real or faux)

Creating the Main Tree Trunk

1. Support both ends of the 4 inch round PVC pipe. Two ladders work well for this. Choose the first bend spot about two feet from bottom. The bottom trunk should remain fairly straight in order to use the support pole later. Small bends can be used.

10 foot PVC - 4 inch round

2. Using a heat gun close to surface, move heat gun back and forth until the PVC is begins to get soft. Begin applying pressure with other hand to the PVC just outside the heated area.

3. Once the PVC bends desired amount, maintain pressure on both sides of the spot for at least one minute. Place a wet rag over heated area to cool down faster.

4. Rotate the main trunk PVC to make the next bend about 12 inches from the first and on a different side. The goal is a natural tree silhouette with bends and angles, not a straight pole.

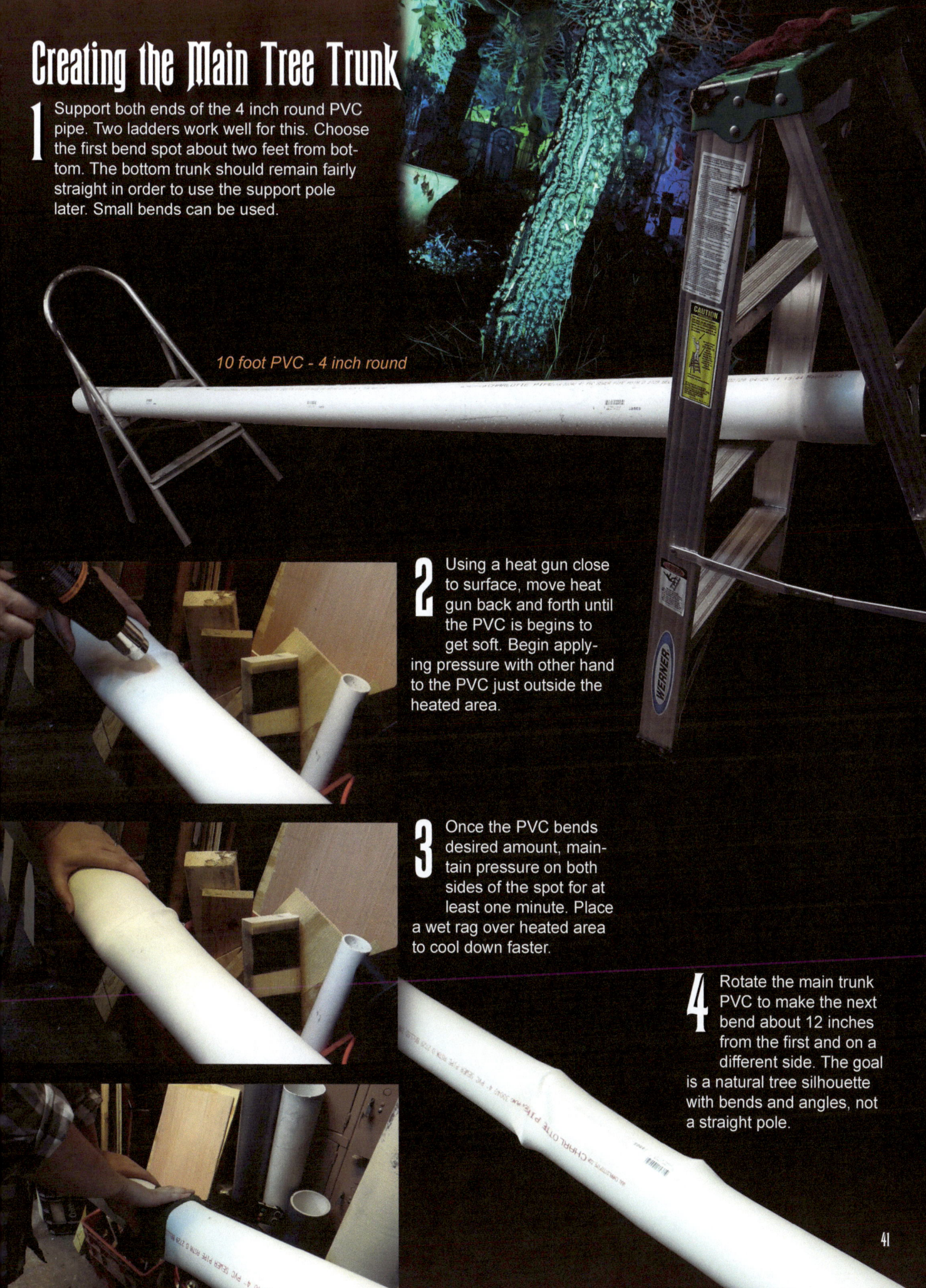

Creating the Main Branches

Clamps to flatten PVC branch ends.

1 Create anywhere from 3 to 5 main branches for the top half of the tree. Use a PVC cutter or saw to cut random lengths for the main branches.

2 Use the heat gun to heat one end of each PVC branch. Once soft, clamp to create a flattened end. Set aside until cool.

3 Depending on how long the branch is, use a heat gun to shape several bends in the branch as shown. Use a wet rag to speed up cooling the PVC bent angle before moving to the next.

4 Once all the branches are shaped, pre-drill two 1/8 inch holes in the flat end of each branch.

Creating Secondary Branches

1 Create 1 or 2 secondary branches for each main branch. These should be around 6 – 10 inches in length. Use PVC cutters to cut desired lengths.

2 Use the heat gun to heat one end of each PVC branch. Once soft, clamp to create a flattened end. Set aside until cool.

3 Depending on how long the branch is, use a heat gun to shape several bends in the branch as shown. Use a wet rag to speed up cooling the PVC bent angle before moving to the next.

4 Use screws to attach to the main branches. Alternate the sides they branch out. They could point up or down depending on the look you want.

5 The main branches should be placed on alternating sides of the top half of the main trunk. Attach using screws in the pre-drilled holes.

43

Creating the Tree Texture

1 Tree texture can be applied with tree standing up or lying down. To stand up tree, hammer the metal pole two feet into the ground. Place your tree over the metal pole. It should be secure enough that it can't be easily pushed over. Apply spray foam using the straw supplied. Do not pre-shake the can. Run lines of foam in vertical lines along trunk and branches. Leave space between each line. As it hardens go back and fill in the spaces. This helps to apply the foam lines and keep them from falling off. Tiny gaps are fine, but the texture should nearly cover the entire surface of the PVC in the end. This will help keep it from coming off the PVC.

2 Once the tree is completely covered in foam, let sit overnight or more. The foam will continue to expand slightly even days later. If you don't want any of the yellow foam to show through your paint, let the tree sit for at least a week before painting.

TIP: Before hammering metal poles into ground, be sure and check with the city to find out where any utilities pipes might exist.

Metal Pole

3. Paint the entire tree using black, exterior house paint. Get down into every nook and crevice. Let dry overnight.

4. Use a dry brush to lightly brush over the top parts of the texture using brown, craft paint. This will highlight the texture. Let dry.

5. Hammer the metal pole 2 feet into the ground at the final resting place for the tree. Place tree bottom over the pole.

6. Insert lightweight real tree branches into some of the opening of the PVC branches to extend the height of the tree even more. Hang Spanish moss, spider webs, or add props to tree to complete the look.

Brown Paint Applied

Hang Spanish moss, spider webs, or add props to tree to complete the look.

Filler Spiders
Fill Those Webs with these...

If you are doing any kind of spider theme, you will need a lot of BIG spiders. It's not very cost effective to buy a ton of giant spiders when you might only want to use them a few times. We had just that dilemma in our Invasion of the Spiders. We needed some big, filler spiders to populate our giant spider webs and we needed to be able to make them fast and lightweight. This is the solution we came up with.

YOU WILL NEED: 12-14 inch round plastic ball for each spider, black, plastic, contractor bags, strong wire, hot glue gun, glue sticks, black pipe cleaners, black duct tape, black, hairy yarn, collections of plastic grocery bags, black pipe foam insulation, ping pong balls, planter liners made of coco hair, black spray paint, wooden paint stick or yard stick, scissors, utility knife, wire cutters

Prep Work

Cut one inch strips of plastic ties out of the plastic contractor bags. Set aside.

Use a utility knife to cut the ping pong balls in half. Spray paint them with black spray paint. Each spider will need four eyes. Let dry.

Spray paint in black the wooden paint stick or yard stick. Let dry.

Take the planter liner and shred into small chunks. This is best done outside. It is very messy!

Cut strips of contractor garbage bags

Shredded coco planter liner

Plastic Grocery Bags

Kid's Ball

Black Pipe Foam Insulation

Cut strips of contractor garbage bags

Strong Wire

Ping Pong Balls

Black Duct Tape

Hot Glue Gun

Contractor Strength Bags

Pipe Cleaners

Shredded Coco Liner

Fancy Yarn

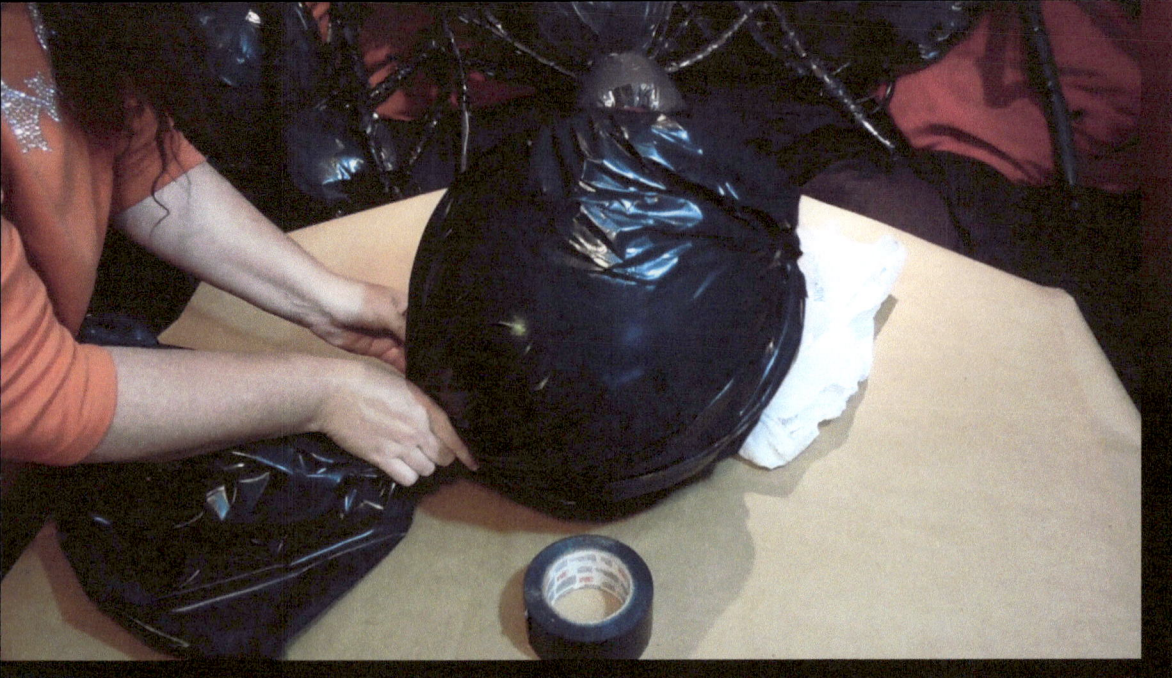

1. Build the body: Place the ball inside a new contractor bag. Take the two ends at the back of the ball and tie them together. Tuck the ends inside the tie. Hold the open bag end and press the air out of the bag. Use pipe cleaner to twist bag closed.

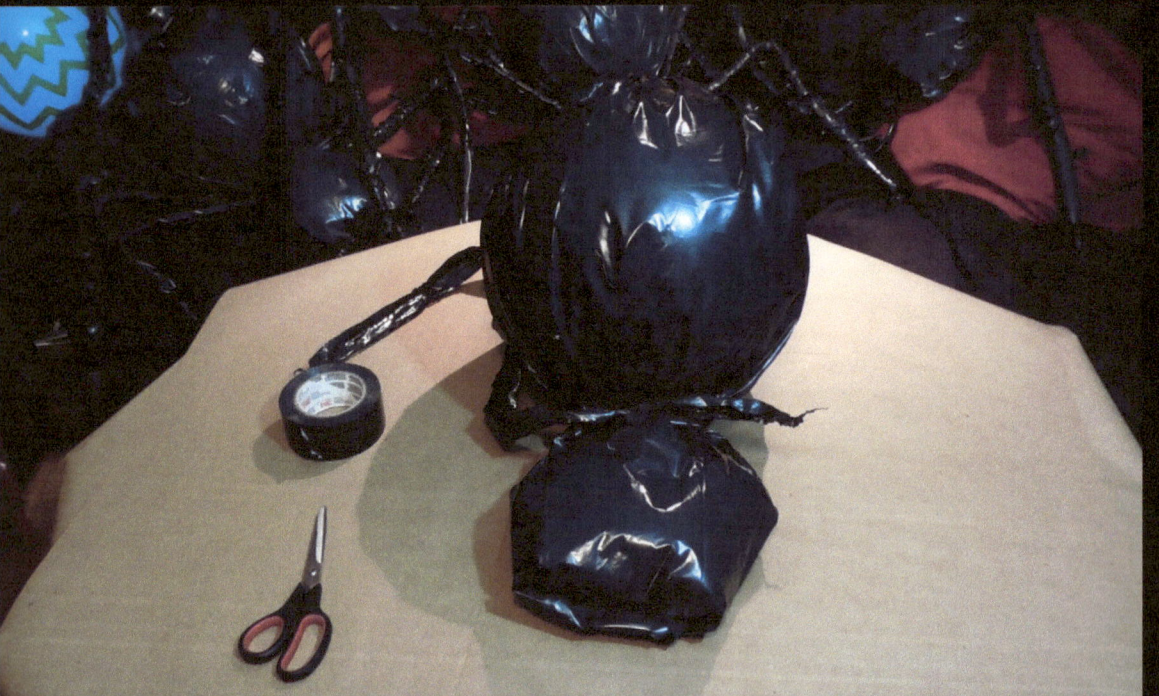

2. With remaining open bag portion, stuff with several small, plastic bags. Create a flattened head shape. Fold edges under and tape underneath. To keep the body and head in position, use a 1 inch plastic strip to tie body to back of head. Use scissors to make a small hole in plastic around body near each side of head. Slip the tie through the holes and tie off. Then tie around neck area.

3. To create spider pinchers, cut a 10 inch piece of wire. Bend into a U shape. Attach some scrap foam or insulation pieces and cover with black duct tape along the entire surface. Pull tighter at both ends so it is more pointed.

4 Tie a 1 inch plastic strip to the side of the pincher. Cut a small hole into the head near the front side. Slip the tie through and tie off. Do same for other side.

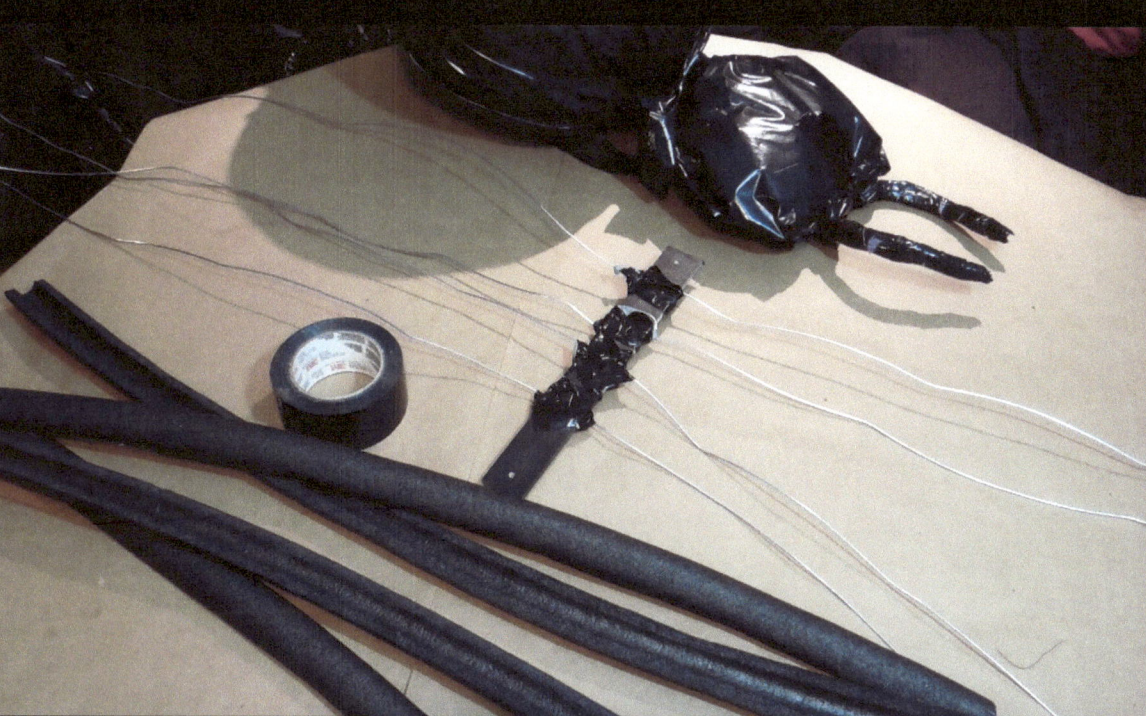

5 Use wire cutters to cut 4 pieces of 68 inch long wire. Bend each wire in half. Twist once around the wooden stick. Tape in place. Leave about 2 inches between each wire and attach each the same way. Drill a small hole (for a hook) in the body end of the stick.

6 The pipe insulation has a cut along the entire length. Open this and cut the length in half again along the length. Then cut the pipe insulation to fit each wire leg extension. Tape each piece at a few spots along the wire just to hold it in place.

7 Using 1 inch plastic strips, tie off at the start of each leg (next to wooden stick). Braid the plastic down the length of the leg. Tie off at the end of each piece and continue with more plastic strips until each leg is complete.

8 Place the spider body on top of the wood stick. Use plastic tie to attach body to wooden stick at neck. Turn spider around and add another tie to end of wooden stick.

9 Cut two small holes in plastic of spider body. Slip tie through holes and tie to stick. Wrap tie around back legs and tie to stick again. Bend wire legs in center of each to shape.

10 Bend a small piece of wire into a hook shape and place in hole at back of stick. Hang the spider in the web, bending the wire legs as needed to pose.

Bottom of Completed Body

Lynne bends the spider legs into shape.

Completed Body Structure

11 This next step require a light touch! Hot glue, piece by piece, the shredded the coco liner to the spider body, head, and legs. When hot gluing the body (ball) there is the risk of popping the ball from the heat of the glue. Lay the clump of hair down and apply the hot glue to a few points on it, then apply lightly to the body. It doesn't take much glue to hold it to the body.

12 Wrap each spider fang with the fancy yarn. Hot glue ends to keep in place.

13 Attach the spider eyes using hot glue.

Lynne works on the Spider.

Completed Spider

Hot glue the coco hair to top surface of each leg.

Spider seen at night.

Hot Glue the Spider Eyes in place.

Completed Spider Eyes and Fangs

Shawn tests out the new spider!

YOU WILL NEED: Beef netting (however many pounds needed), utility knife, scissors, white nylon rope, metal ring (any size), two screws and a drill

Beef Netting Spider Webs

Beef netting is a newer material being used by home haunters. It is actually used to wrap meat in processing plants. The netting is purchased by the pound and comes on a roll in tube form. It must be first cut in half to create flat panels. Once cut, the length can be cut as needed. It weathers well and will get whiter after being in the sun a while. The edges, where cut, will also fray slightly, which looks good in the haunt setting! Beef netting webs are also reusable and easy to store. Just bunch it up and store it in a container for next year.

To Cut a Beef Netting Panel

1 Unroll a length of beef netting. Cut length needed. Cut tube in half to create panel.

2 Add two screws to the top of a door frame or fence about 24 inches apart.

3 Place top edges of beef netting onto the screws. Pull material taunt. If long enough, stand on the bottom edge.

4 Use utility knife to cut as many holes as needed. CAUTION! Do not do this around kids or pets and be careful cutting the holes!

To do both our front and back yard we used a total of 70 pound of beef netting.

There are two types of cut beef netting panels we like to use in our haunt. One is cut so it is entirely made of holes. Once in place larger holes can be cut in to allow better views through in certain spots where a scene might need more visibly.

The second cut style is more opaque. This beef netting panel can be used to conceal parts of your scene or help a prop stand out more from its background. One excellent use is to hide lights from the audiences' front view.

Beef Netting comes on a roll

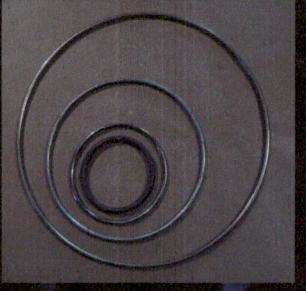

To create a large focal spider web or when hanging a HUGE web overhead, build a rope support structure first. Use a metal ring for the central web point. Any size ring will do. Tie a rope to the ring and take it to the first connection and tie off. Then do same for the opposite side. Once the main lines are run, tie a few in between ropes around the central ring just as a real spider web would do. Attach the beef netting panels each angling toward the central ring.

When hanging the beef netting panels layering is key. Pull a corner to the first connection point and tie off. Pull an opposite corner and tie off. If a corner doesn't reach, cut a thin 1 inch strip out of extra beef netting to use as a rope. Tie this to the end point on the panel then to the connection point. Panels can be tied together to make wider sections. Beef netting can be dropped from roof lines, draped over trees, attached to bricks, or wrapped around captured victims. A little web imagination is all that is needed.

When any lights are placed behind the webs they seem to glow at night! Use a variety of colors for a magical effect or white lights to really show off the webs.

For overhead webs the beef netting will drape downward between the rope supports. Whether seen from below or above, the effect is pretty cool. Be sure to add lots of spiders!

Motion Activated Spider

YOU WILL NEED: 4x4 foot wood panel (at least 1/2 inch thick), 2x4 blocks, black, plastic contractor bags, heavy gauge wire, PVC ½ inch round, black pipe insulation, heat gun, drill, 1 ¼ hole drill bit, screws, ¼ inch threaded rod cut down to 2 inch pieces for 8 rods, ¼ nuts, 3/8 inch One Hole Straps (16 pieces), wind shield wiper motor, 2 – 5 inch pulley wheels, 1 – ¼ inch Coupling Nut, 1 – ¼ rounded head screw, 2 flat metal pieces (needs to fit the width of both wheels), 2 long ¼ bolts & nut, wire cutters, spray foam, 1 large plastic ornament container (comes apart for 2 halves), 2 ping pong balls (cut in half), Monster Guts Pacemaker (*NOTE: Monster Guts Pacemaker has been replaced by PWM DC Motor Speed Controller*), or other voltage controller, 28 inch plastic beach ball (or largest you can find), black duct tape, 2 coco planter lines (shredded), motion detector with two plugs (re-wired so it can be plugged in), large shot light, green shop light bulb, prop to cover the motion detector, zip ties, black spray paint, Gorilla Glue

Nothing could be creepier than a giant 8 foot spider... except one that also moved when you approach it! We found the inspiration for this project online but made a few modifications and made it much, much bigger for our haunt. We also added a motion detector trigger so a light comes on and the motor turns on causing all the legs to move independently. Because the end of each leg is wire the legs flop around a lot more and the effect is even creepier!

TOP VIEW

1 Cut a shape similar to the one shown here from the 4 x4 board. Attach using screws 3 -- 2x4 blocks for feet as shown in side view. Mark out the center point in the leg area. Drill 4 evenly spaced holes at least ½ inch from edge for each leg. View step 7 before cutting holes! The assembled wheel piece needs to overlap the holes from the center point for the legs to move.

2 Cut the threaded rod down to 8 pieces each two inches in length.

3 Cut the 8 PVC legs 33.5 inches long. Use a heat gun to shape as shown. Drill ¼ inch hole in both ends of leg at side points. Next, cut a wire 30 inches long. Insert wire into highest leg hole and twist around several times. Bend wire as shown.

SIDE VIEW

5 1/8 inch high

Use at least 1/2 inch thick base wood

Extra strong contractor bags are used for a variety of parts and projects

Put wire through hole then twist about PVC for support

PVC leg bends up and wire bends down to for each spider leg

30 inch wire

33.5 inch PVC leg

3.5 inches to hole

4 Wrap a length of foam insulation along leg leaving the first bend free. At end of leg, bend the access foam material under to create a padded foot. Braid a 1 inch strip of plastic (cut from contractor's plastic bags) down entire length of leg and tie around foot several times. Cover with coco hair attached with hot glue. Leave the first 3.5 inches of legs clear.

Spider Foot Detail

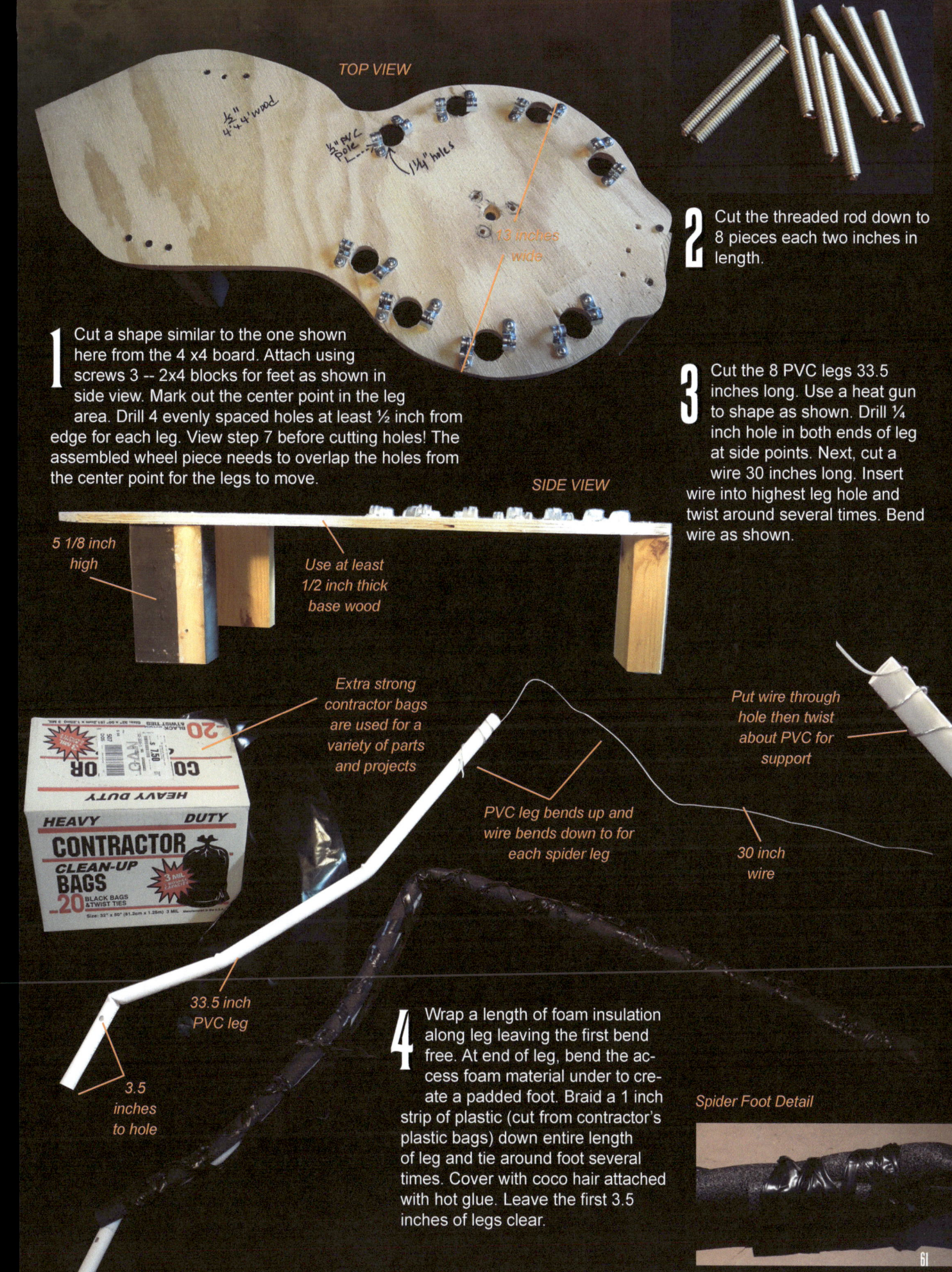

NOTE: We found that after the motion activated spider was run for an evening, the leg movements tended to knock the rods and bolts out of place. To fix this we placed screws on the outside points of each rod to keep it from shifting.

One completed leg structure

5 Insert each leg start hole with threaded rod. Place this in hole of wooden base. Add a nut to end side of threaded rod near ends of rod. Screw One Hole Straps on each side over the nuts and into the wood. The leg should be able to pivot freely.

6 Drill a ¼ hole in the center of the wooden base (for the motor arm). Cut a second hole in center of body area (for the motor connector wire to go through to the voltage controller).

NOTE: Monster Guts Pacemaker has been replaced by PWM DC Motor Speed Controller

7 Using scrap wood, create a shelf underneath the body area, between the two support feet to create a shelf. This is for the Pacemaker, or voltage controller to sit. This is where the spider is turned on.

Shawn tests out the spider leg movements.

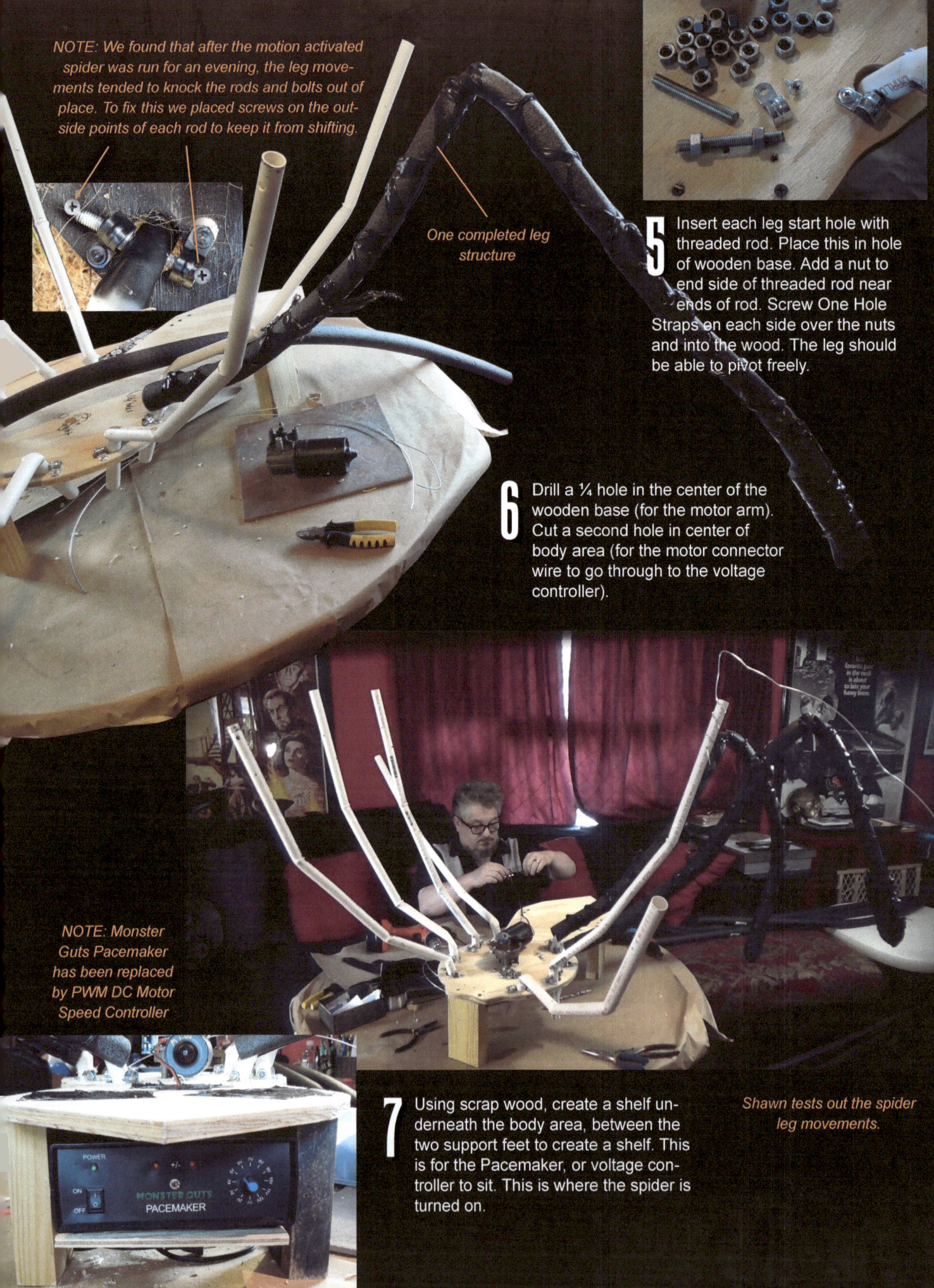

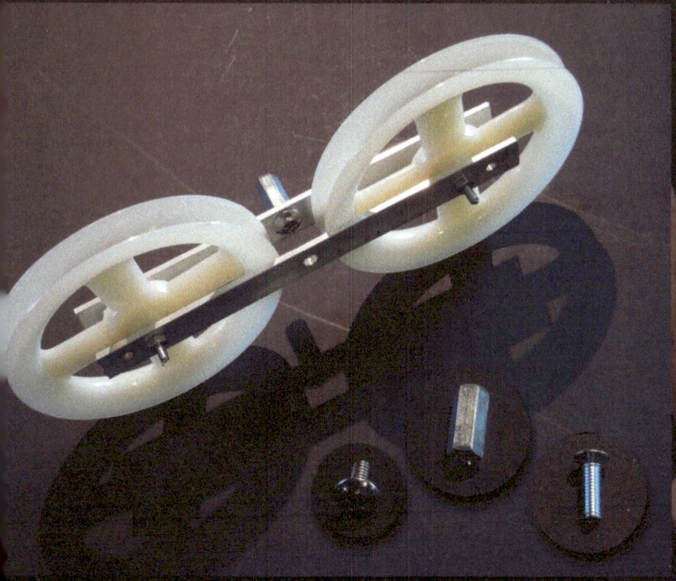

8 Assemble the wheels using two flat metal pieces. Drill 3 holes in each as shown. Use bolt and nuts through each metal piece with wheels in-between. Attach ¼ inch Coupling Nut and ¼ rounded head screw in one of the center holes as shown. This is placed in center hole in wood and attached to motor. Use flat head screws to attach motor to wood. As the motor turns the wheel section the PVC legs are pushed away causing them to move upwards on the reverse side.

9 Run the motor connector wire through the body section hole and underneath to the Pacemaker or voltage controller. Drill two small holes on either side of wire and zip tie down so it doesn't get caught on any of the moving legs. Plug in and test.

Wind shield wiper motor

Zip tie secures connector wire

Hole for connector wire

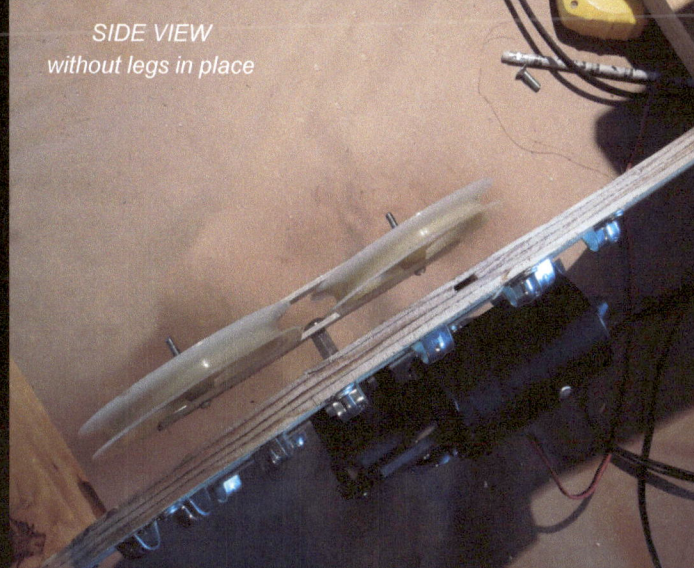

SIDE VIEW
without legs in place

28 inch ball

21 inches wide

7 inches high

11 Cut a second wooden oval for the ball to sit on. Attach two 2x4 on each side. This whole piece should sit over the main base back section. Having it as a separate piece allows for adjustments. If the body is too close to the legs it will prevent them from moving. Spray paint wood with black. Tie the ball to the board through two cut holes. Tie off.

10 Blow up the beach ball. Cover the ball with several plastic contractor bags. They may need to be cut apart and taped down. Do at least 2 layers of plastic. Attach two ties one on each side of the ball. Cover with coco hair attached with hot glue.

12 Gorilla glue three 2x4 wood blocks on sides and front of motor allowing the legs to still pivot. This is to allow the mid-section cover to have a place to sit, while allowing the moving legs parts to work and protecting the motor area.

13 Create flat head shape by stuffing a contractor bag with several plastic bags. Fold ends under and tape down. Cover with coco hair attached with hot glue. Attach with screws and ties to front wood block.

14 Spider Eyes: Cut the ping pong balls in half. Open two halves of the plastic ornament. Spray paint the inside of all. Let dry. Attach with hot glue to head.

5 inch long 2x4. Mid-section gets attached to these blocks.

3.5 inch long 2x4. Head gets screwed to this block.

16 Motion Detector: re-wire a motion detector light as a plug-in light. Plug in the shop light and the Pacemaker (voltage controller). Hide the motion detector under a prop near where people will be walking and to protect it from moisture. As person approaches both the light and the motor will be activated.

Motion Detector is hiden under urn. As guest approached fence, the spider comes ALIVE!

15 The mid-section body part is made from spray foam. To create: put a sheet of plastic wrap on a flat surface. Spray foam a filled rectangle shape that will fit the length of the motor area. Let dry. Spray paint black. Fit into place over motor. Pull off some of the side bits in order for the legs to move freely. Attach by screws to the wooden blocks on either side of the motor. Cover with coco hair attached with hot glue.

17 inch long mid-section

Web Victims

YOU WILL NEED: plastic shopping bags, one piece jumpers (various kid sizes), plastic air bags bodies (optional body form as seen in Chapter One), various kids costumes, masks, trick-or-treat bags or buckets, beef netting spider webs panels, mirror ball motors (optional for turning figures)

The Trick-or-Treaters That Didn't Get Away!

They were big spiders with giant appetites! And the only thing they had on their minds were all those trick-or-treaters who so willingly wandered right into their web… Everywhere one looked there were costumed bundles of web-wrapped treats.

Body Form

Mask & Cowboy Hat

Monster Cowboy

Ties at joints help to pose character once in costume.

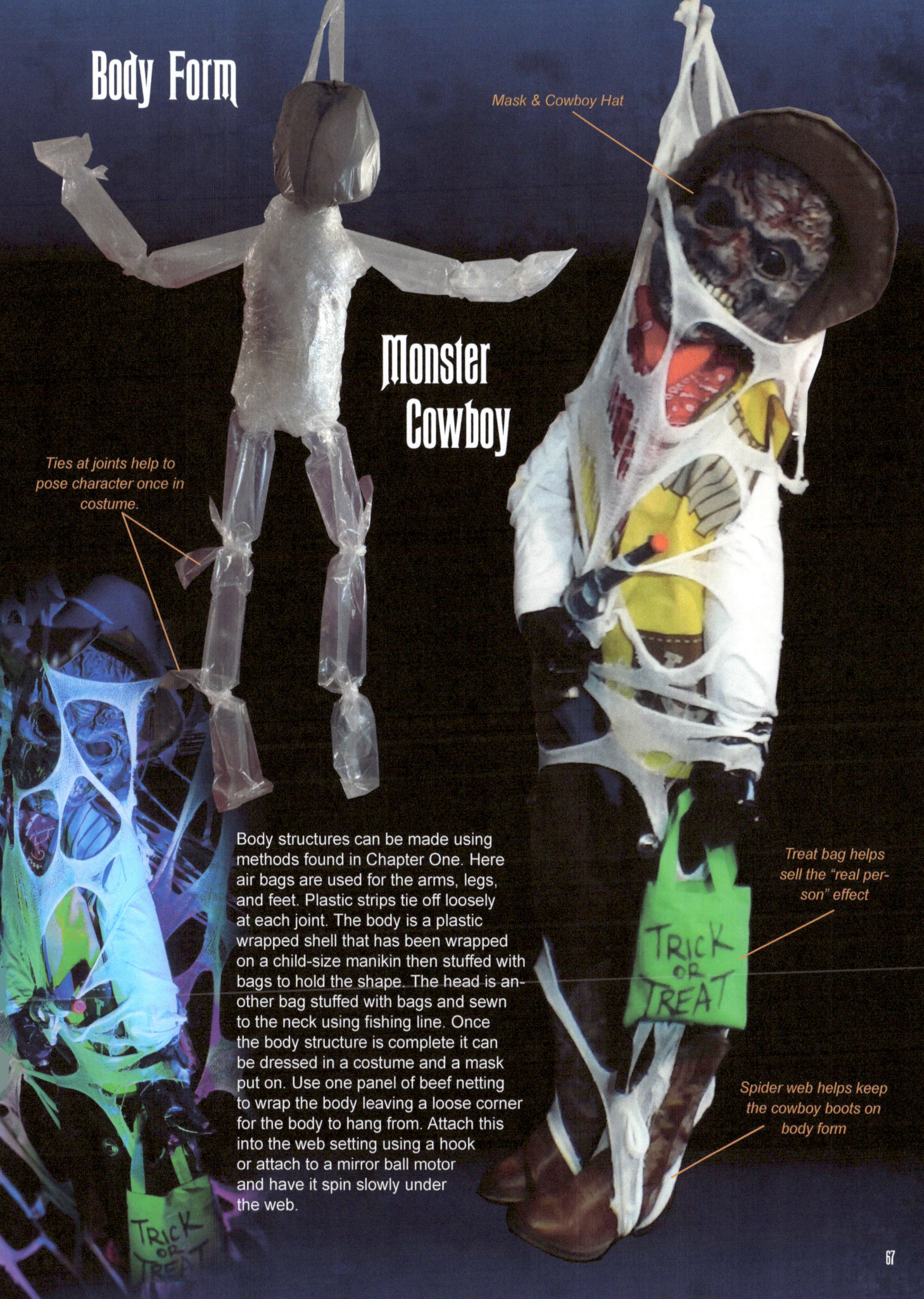

Body structures can be made using methods found in Chapter One. Here air bags are used for the arms, legs, and feet. Plastic strips tie off loosely at each joint. The body is a plastic wrapped shell that has been wrapped on a child-size manikin then stuffed with bags to hold the shape. The head is another bag stuffed with bags and sewn to the neck using fishing line. Once the body structure is complete it can be dressed in a costume and a mask put on. Use one panel of beef netting to wrap the body leaving a loose corner for the body to hang from. Attach this into the web setting using a hook or attach to a mirror ball motor and have it spin slowly under the web.

Treat bag helps sell the "real person" effect

Spider web helps keep the cowboy boots on body form

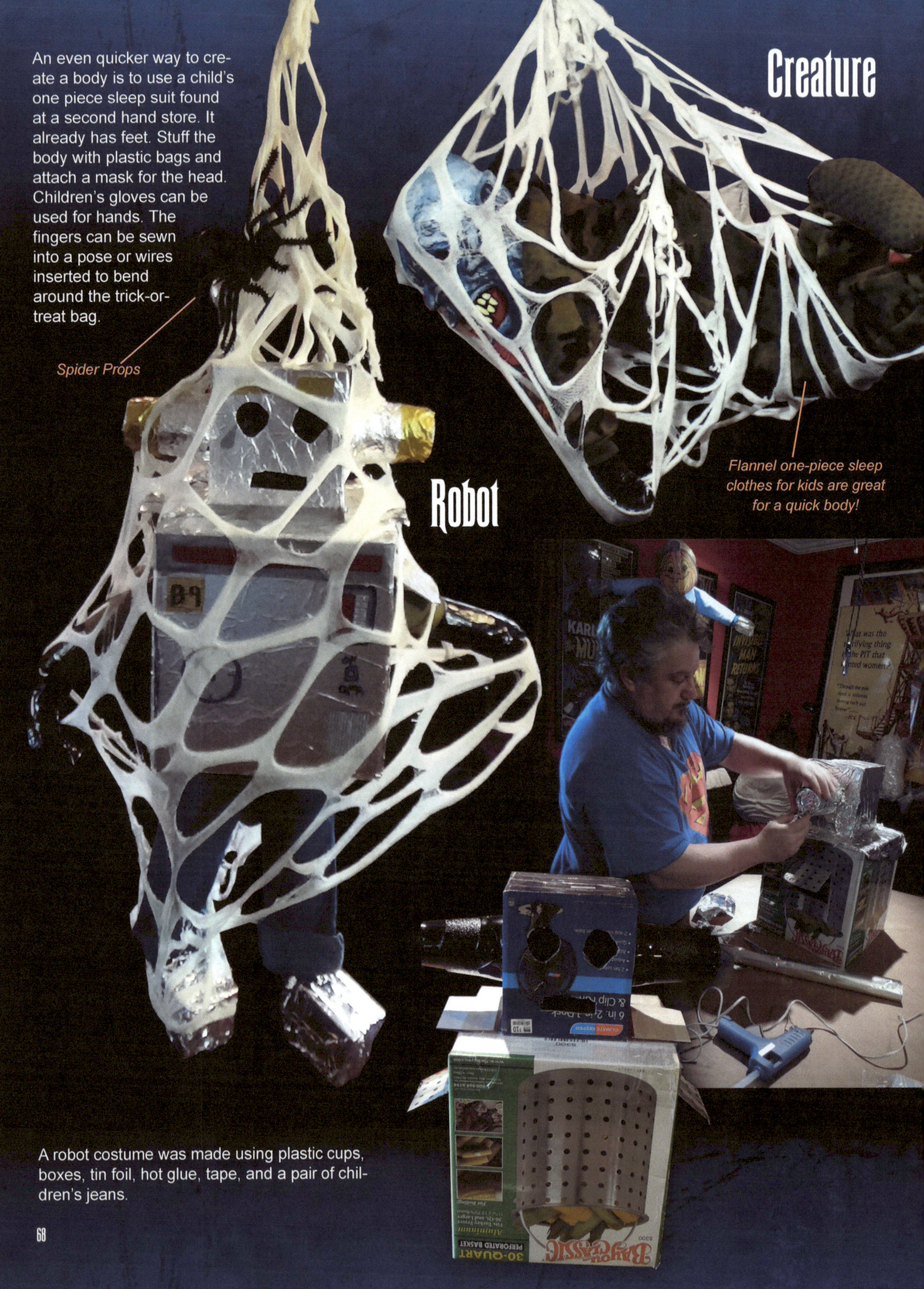

An even quicker way to create a body is to use a child's one piece sleep suit found at a second hand store. It already has feet. Stuff the body with plastic bags and attach a mask for the head. Children's gloves can be used for hands. The fingers can be sewn into a pose or wires inserted to bend around the trick-or-treat bag.

Spider Props

Creature

Flannel one-piece sleep clothes for kids are great for a quick body!

Robot

A robot costume was made using plastic cups, boxes, tin foil, hot glue, tape, and a pair of children's jeans.

Jointed-Leg Spider

These giant webs are made by giant spiders!

YOU WILL NEED: Several cans of expanding foam (Great Stuff), 1/2 PVC tubes cut in various sizes, 8 PVC angle connectors, drill and 1/4 inch drill bit, heat gun, clamps, 1/4 hole washers, 1/4 bolts, 1/4 key nuts or 1/4 lock nuts, wood for body base, twine rope, black spray paint, black duct tape, plastic blow-up beach ball, hot glue gun and sticks, saran wrap (Glad Press'n Seal), tape, panty hose, clear plastic fill-able Christmas ornaments (for eyes) or other lens-like eye parts, black and brown hairy yarns, small piece of plastic, needle and thread, wire, plastic bags (or other stuffing)

Nothing is more creepy than spiders. Except maybe, bigger spiders.... Much, much, bigger spiders! The kind that dine on pets, people and trick-or-treaters!

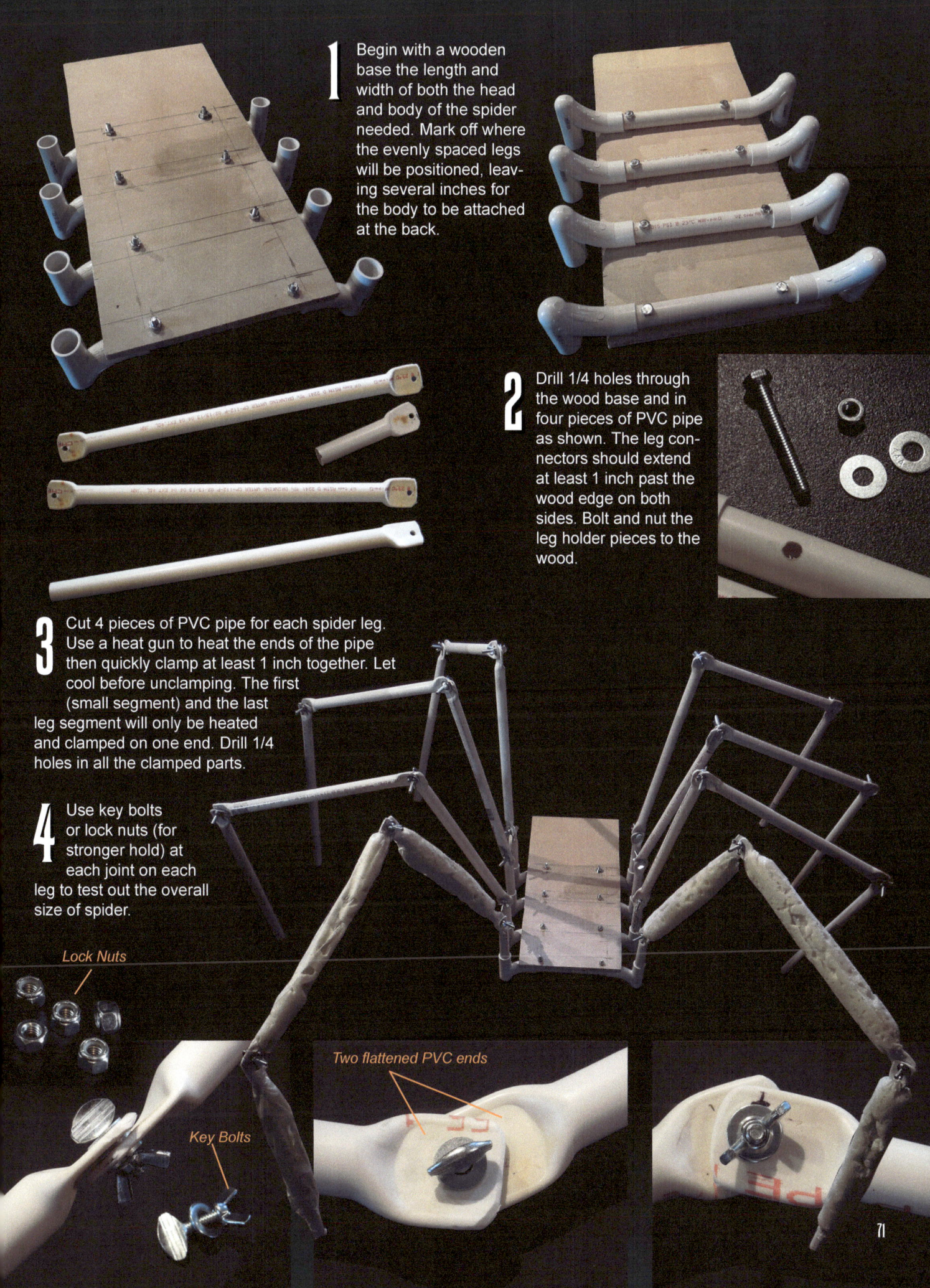

5 To create the creepy spider leg texture you will need 3 things. Press'n seal plastic wrap, tape, and expandable spray foam.

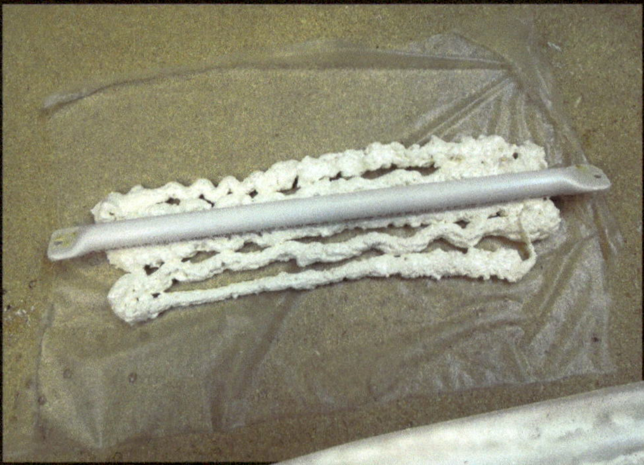

6 Cut out a length of plastic wrap the length of one leg segment. Spray several rows of foam on to the plastic wrap. This should be shorter than the leg and not cover the leg ends. Place the leg segment on top of the foam. Carefully pull up the plastic wrap so it loosely surrounds the leg. There may be some gaps in the foam. This is OK. Tape the ends of the leg segment tightly so no foam will expand in these areas. Lean the package at an angle against a wall and let it set overnight.

Plastic wrap is loosely applied over the spray foam and taped off on ends.

7 Unwrap the leg segments. Peel off as much of the plastic as possible. If the leg bulk is not enough, you can do the process again over the dried foam, or simply spray some onto the leg and let harden. We were going for a somewhat deteriorating, creepy look, so having some chunks missing were ok.

8 Once the leg segment size works, spray paint the segments with black spray paint. Let dry.

9 To form the spider body blow up a beach ball that is the of the spider body. Cover each side with spray foam. Be sure to leave a clear, uncovered area around the air release valve on one end. Let harden, then cover the remaining sides. Once the foam has expanded and hardened, release the ball air and carefully remove the ball.

10 Spray paint the spider body with black spray paint.

11 Trim the back end of the wooden base so it is curved as shown. Drill two 1/4 inch holes just past the last leg segments in the base. Cut a piece of plastic that is slightly wider than the holes. Add matching holes in the plastic.

12 Place the plastic inside the spider body close to the opening. The plastic is used to keep the bolts from tearing through the spray foam body after being attached to the board. Spray paint both sides of the wooden base and the leg connectors. Do not paint inside the leg connectors!

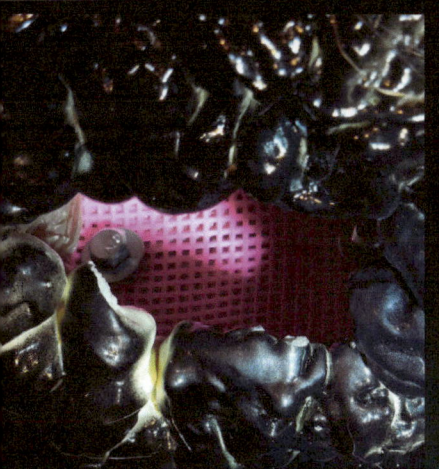

13 The Spider Head: Cut off the legs of a pair of panty hose. Knot the leg openings. Stuff the inside with plastic bags. Spray paint with black. Let dry.

Ping pong balls can also be used for eyes. Simply cut in half and spray paint.

14 Open the plastic Christmas ornament holder into two parts. These will be the two larger spider eyes. For the two smaller eyes we used children's toy spy scopes, but you can use anything you want, including smaller Christmas ornament holders. Spray paint the inside of the eyes (or outside, as needed) in black and let dry.

15 Use "hairy" yarns in black and brown to over the spider's head.

16 Hot glue the eyes in place. Cover the head in the yarns using hot glue. Careful not to touch the hot glue! Use a toothpick or stick to help lay down the yarn strands.

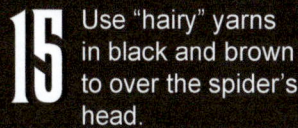

Alternate spider "hair" can be made from coco planter box liners, as in the Filler Spiders Chapter.

18 Cut a second pair of panty hose by removing the legs. Fit this over the wooden base, cutting holes for each of the leg connectors. Stuff with a few plastic bags to add a little bulk. Spray paint black. Let dry.

17 Spider fangs and Pedipalp (two short leg parts next to fangs): The fangs were created with bent wire, wrapped in plastic bag, covered in black duct tape which tapered at fang ends. Black "hairy" yarn is wrapped around the fangs toward back end to add some bulk. Two wire loops were left at center to be able to attach to wooden base. The pedipalp is created with PVC pipe that has been heated with heat gun and bent slightly. Cover with expanding foam and wipe down with stick to get smaller texture. Let harden. Spray paint black. Wrap sparingly with hairy yarn that is hot glued in place. Drill 1/4 inch holes in end to bolt to wooden base.

19 Stitch head to this body pad at sides just to hold in place.

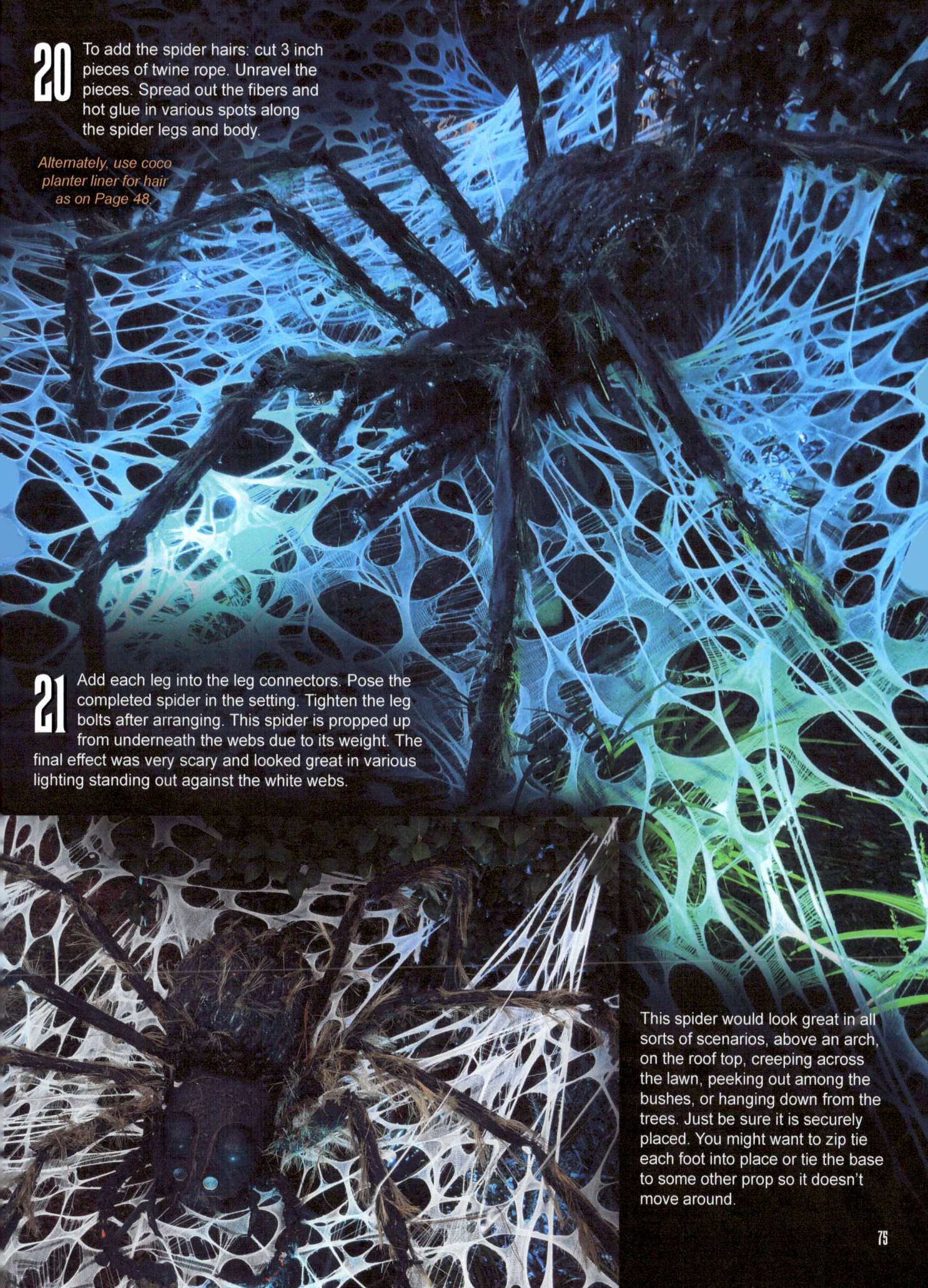

20 To add the spider hairs: cut 3 inch pieces of twine rope. Unravel the pieces. Spread out the fibers and hot glue in various spots along the spider legs and body.

Alternately, use coco planter liner for hair as on Page 48.

21 Add each leg into the leg connectors. Pose the completed spider in the setting. Tighten the leg bolts after arranging. This spider is propped up from underneath the webs due to its weight. The final effect was very scary and looked great in various lighting standing out against the white webs.

This spider would look great in all sorts of scenarios, above an arch, on the roof top, creeping across the lawn, peeking out among the bushes, or hanging down from the trees. Just be sure it is securely placed. You might want to zip tie each foot into place or tie the base to some other prop so it doesn't move around.

What Created the Giant Spiders?
Toxic Scene

YOU WILL NEED: 24 inch board to attach all parts, two wood blocks, windshield wiper motor, Monster Guts – Pacemaker (*NOTE: Monster Guts Pacemaker has been replaced by PWM DC Motor Speed Controller*) OR Voltage Adapter to adjust speed of motor, two PVC legs, heat gun & clamps, small chain, key rings, screws, drill, washers & metal spacers, flat metal bars or flat metal bracket, adjustable double sided eye hooks, small eye screws, C Clamps, small bolts & nuts, ½ inch L Brackets, Spray Foam, black spray paint, green and yellow florescent spray paint, spider leg "hair" (rope or coco planter fibers), black trash cans, toxic labels, black duct tape, bubble maker, bubble juice, green shop light, utility knife, black zip ties, bucket with lid, black flex hose, fog machine, PVC pipe with 90 angle to fit end of fog machine

Kicking Spider Legs Motor Project

This project is based on the Kicking Legs motor projects found online in the home haunt community. Instead of two human legs kicking, we turned the PVC "legs" upside down and made them into two spider legs sticking out of a toxic barrel! We also used Monster Guts, Pacemaker in order to slow down the speed of the windshield wiper motor.

NOTE: Monster Guts Pacemaker has been replaced by PWM DC Motor Speed Controller

1 The base board is lifted on the front end with a wooden block. A second wooden block is used to level off the metal bars rotation point so it is level with the motor arm. Chains connected to both ends of the second metal bar are then connected to each leg lifting it in turn.

2 Each leg chain is connected to a key ring and a double sided adjustable eye hook. These are then connected to another key ring and a small eye hook screwed into the top facing surface of each leg. Some experimenting is required to figure out how much length is needed to reach each leg. Use the adjustable eye hook to shorten or lengthen the amount.

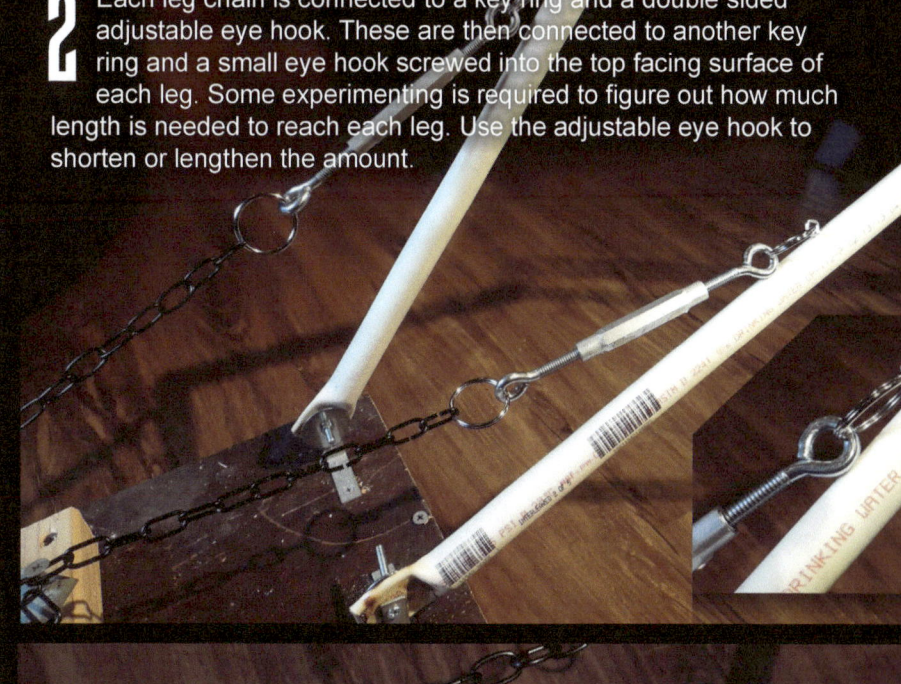

3 On the first metal bar, drill approximately 3/8 inch holes in each end. The first hole connects with the motor arm. For the second hole, use washers on top and bottom and through the end hole of the second metal bar and connect all using a pin. Attach chain ends to the second metal plate at each side.

4 A variety of spacers were used to make the metal bars level with the motor arm. A long screw runs from the center of the second metal plate and into the wood block. It should rotate freely.

6 Motor is held to wood base using C Clamps and screws. First metal bar hole is placed over motor arm nut. If adjustments are needed (as shown here) drill more holes in metal end until the right placement is achieved.

5 Each PVC leg is flattened one end using a heat gun and clamps. Drill a ¼ inch hold in center of each flattened part. Screw L brackets on either side of legs with a little space in between. Place washers on each side of flattened parts. Use a bolt and nut to hold in place. Legs should be able to pivot easily..

7 Spray foam each leg, careful not to cover the ends or eye hooks. Let dry.

8 Two more static spider legs can be placed on either side of the base board for effect.

9 Once spray foam is set, spray paint black. Let dry. Hot glue either rope hair or planter liner hair down the length of each leg.

Toxic Barrel Bubbler

Toxic barrels are made from large black trash cans. Spray foam around top in several passes. Let dry. Then spray paint green and yellow fluorescent paints. Let dry. Add variety of toxic stickers to can sides. For toxic barrels that are standing upright place a bubble maker such as this one inside with a light.

For the spider leg kicker the toxic spray foam was made in two parts to help conceal the inner workings of the spider legs and allow for adjustments. Zip tie a green light above the kicker to the top of the trash can.

Cut 2 holes in back end of trash can. One to run any electrical cords out. The second to attach the black flex hose for the fog machine. Use black duct tape to seal flex tube to trash can.

Inside of the Spider Leg Kicker garbage can. Light is zip tied to top in back.

The fog added to the eerie scene!

Testing the fog during the day.

Ice surrounding PVC pipe

Small Chiller

Toxic Barrel Bubbler

Toxic Barrel Bubbler

Small Chiller

PVC pipe from Chiller to Fog Machine

Pacemaker / Speed controller device

Tube that sends chilled fog into Leg Kicker can.

Fog Machine

Toxic Barrel Fogger

Small bucket chiller with PVC pipe inserted into one side with 90 angle inside to release the fog inside the closed bucket. The ice chills the fog and lets it escape out the black flex tube and into the spider kicker toxic can. The effect at night was really great!

Making An Entrance
Invasion of the Spiders!

When the Mitchells' decide to do a 50's B-movie inspired theme of giant spiders… they also have to do a massive amount of giant spider webs! That means 70+ pounds of hand-cut spider webbing that has to be hung, piece by piece, from the roof, the trees, the bushes, and every other thing or person who happened to be around the haunt.

Beef Netting Spider's Web was used for the majority of the scene, but store-bought stretch webbing was also mixed in, going from the roof tops to the tallest bushes for a bit of fine detail.

Don't forget the spiders, whether they are hand-made or store-bought, they are the scary stars of the theme! But, on occasion, even spiders have a sense of humor! The spider on the right was spotted hanging out in a baby carriage with baby bottle in it's mouth and a bib that said, "Dinner's on me".

Spider catches the cat and takes him for a spin...

The path from the entrance is also treacherous and lined with webs. Careful... you may not make it out the other side!

The Mitchells' costumes for a 1950's lady and Acme bug sprayer complete with pre-attached spiders.

Be sure and draw attention a little closer to the street. As cars, buses, and people pass by our house, they catch a good look at what's waiting this year at the Mitchells' house. This large spider waits next to the walkway entrance. He has been busy building his web and now wants to catch someone in it!

Sometimes even we run screaming from our own creations!

Spider's nest filled with hungry, baby spiders!

Disco ball motor rotates web holding figure.

This poor trick-or-treater dressed as Spiderman has two spiders clinging to him as he spins using a disco ball motor. To add to the effect add a flashlight which is turned on in one hand and a trick-or-treat bucket in the other hand.

An unlucky trick-or-treater who didn't make it out of the web!

Setting the Stage: Inside the Haunted House

Candelabras and old portraits will always grace the haunted house walls.

Old photos and paintings are a great collecting hobby for the home haunter. Add some old frames, or new frames made to look old, a few custom cobwebs, the right mood lighting, and any room can be haunt ready instantly!

Boney is always watching those who visit on *All Hallows Eve*.

A Victorian lady still waiting for her love....

Right this way please..... and don't mind the vermin!

Some dressed up battery candles were made by taping a bit of plastic on the ends to add height. Hot glue was then run down all the sides. A mixture of real hot wax and cinnamon was then brushed over the surface for an aging effect.

Anyone call for a séance?

Other Resources

Beef Netting Spider Web material: www.trentonmills.com/halloween_spiderwebs.htm It is purchased by the pound and comes on a large roll. It comes in 5, 10, and 20 pound rolls.

Heat Sealer and Poly Bags:

12" Hand Impulse Sealer - Heat Seal Machine

Place poly bag between seal bars, press down gently and release. Also seals polypropylene and foam.

Poly Tubing Roll less than 10" Width

Poly Tubing can come in a variety of sizes from 2 inch – 6 inch wide. Each roll is around 1075 feet long and up so it can be used on a lot of projects as lightweight filler or quick figure limbs. http://lakelandsupply.com/productbrowseI2.aspx?catid=PTubingSM&lev=3&lv1id=Poly+Bags is an example of one company that sells Poly Tubing.

Both items can also be purchased on Amazon.

www.monsterguts.com For wiper blade motors, quick connects, power supplies, and motor speed control devices- they know what the home haunter needs and makes our lives so much easier!

For more cool Halloween props, special effects and costumes:

www.terrorsyndicate.com, www.scarefactory.com, www.frightcatalog.com, www.darkimaginings.com

Some of the best home haunter forums:

www.hauntspace.com, www.halloween-l.com, www.halloweenforum.com,

www.homehauntersassociation.com
www.garageofevilnetwork.com
www.hauntforum.com

Halloween websites, magazines, and webcast:

www.halloweenalliance.com, www.myscaryhalloween.com, www.homehauntnews.com, www.hauntcast.net

Halloween music:

www.inaworldmusic.net, www.midnightsyndicate.com

Halloween Props and Special FX:

Each year most major retail stores carry some sort of Halloween product displays of the latest props and special effects. As you are making your rounds for new additions to your collection, be sure to check out the craft and fabric stores at the same time. They also carry Halloween items. Don't forget the after Halloween clearance sales. This is a great way to add to your next year's prop arsenal without spending a whole lot of money. If you feel like shopping all year long for Halloween...there are many online shops devoted to Halloween. Doing a search for Halloween prop will get you started. One great resource is

http://www.frightcatalog.com/

Fabric & cheesecloth can be purchased from most fabric stores. Some stores will sell it by the yard. Two online resources:

www.hancockfabrics.com & **www.raglady.com.**

www.ebay.com is also a great online resource for antiques & crafting supplies of all kinds.

Thank You!

We would like to thank everyone who has promoted, read, talked about, purchased, reviewed, been inspired by, and passed on to their kids-- the *How to Haunt Your House* book series! Shawn and I never knew so much could have come from our little Halloween haunt. It started in 2005 with a Halloween party and outdoor cemetery and has grown every year. We have three young additions to our family this year as we are adopting! We hope to inspire them to continue the Halloween home haunt tradition once they are a bit older. Until then, our little monsters must practice with finger paint, construction paper, and the fine art of a glue stick! Stay tuned for more from the new, larger Mitchell family! *The haunting will continue...*

Credits

Font credits: Ravenscroft font was originally conceived and drawn by Tim McKenny, then refined and developed by Justin Callaghan http://www.mickeyavenue.com.

Photos by Shawn and Lynne Mitchell. All projects in this book were used by Shawn and Lynne Mitchell for their Halloween home haunt, *The Mitchell Cemetery & Mausoleum*.

How To Haunt Your House

Home | The Library/Shop | About the Authors | Hack Lab | From the Crypt | Resources | Download | Press | Contact

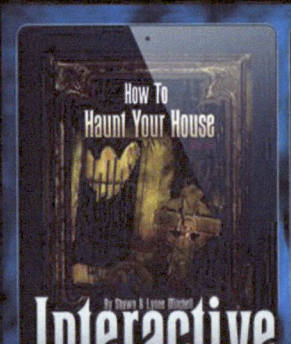 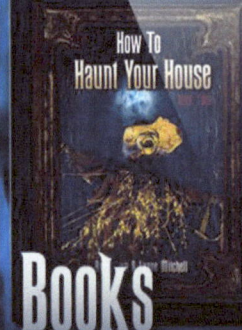 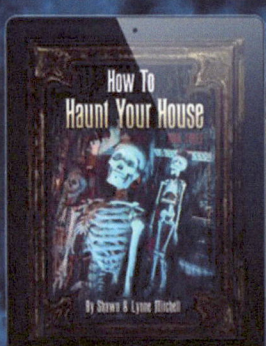 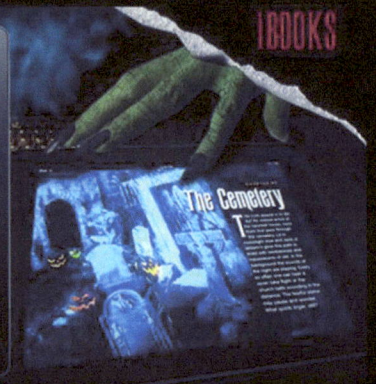

Interactive Books

2014 Mitchell's Halloween Display

Four times the scares... Four times the ghosts... Four times the fun with the Mitchell's, How to Haunt Your House, book series! Keep those Ouija Boards tuned for more-- only the spirits know what they will come up with next!

Visit Us At
WWW.HOWTOHAUNTYOURHOUSE.COM

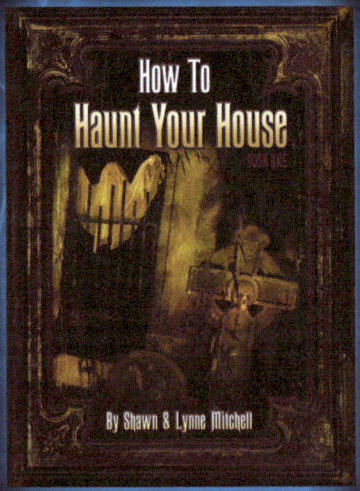  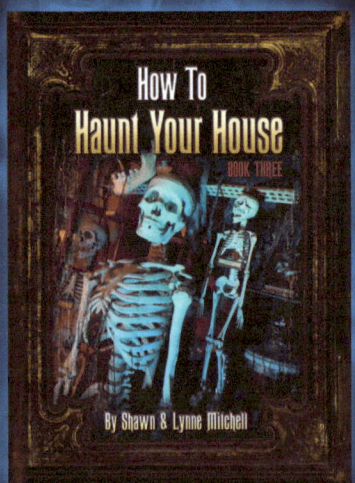 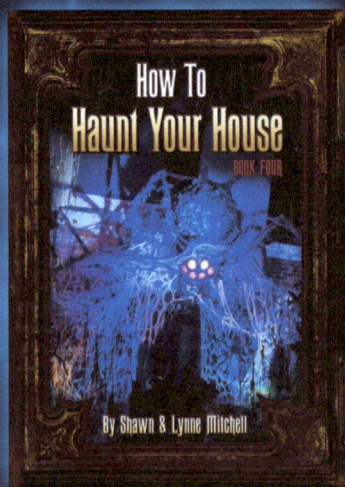

BOOK ONE | BOOK TWO | BOOK THREE | BOOK FOUR

www.ingramcontent.com/pod-product-compliance
Lightning Source LLC
Chambersburg PA
CBHW041403020526
44115CB00036B/10